VATICAN FINANCES

Corrado Pallenberg

VATICAN FINANCES

Peter Owen · London

ISBN O 7206 9401 9

To my wife Peggy

256.72
P178

180440

PETER OWEN LIMITED
12 Kendrick Mews Kendrick Place SW7

First British Commonwealth edition 1971
© 1971 Corrado Pallenberg

Printed in Great Britain by
A. Wheaton & Co Exeter

CONTENTS

In order to facilitate the conversion of figures in this book, it might be useful to mention that at the time of going to press one billion lire was worth about £66,000 or $162,000 and one million lire about £6,600 or $16,200.

INTRODUCTION

'Let not thy left hand know what thy right hand doeth.' This maxim of the Gospel could be taken ironically as a description of the state of Vatican finances today. The confused and confusing situation into which the administration of the Holy See property and funds has drifted can be partly explained, if not entirely justified, by historical vicissitudes, but the situation is further complicated by the many-sidedness of modern Vatican activity.

Besides being the headquarters of a religious body embracing half a billion Christians scattered all over the world, the Vatican is also a great relief agency; a teaching organization running innumerable schools, universities, colleges and seminaries; a cultural organization with eight academies and many more institutes; and an information and propaganda machine with a powerful radio station, newspapers, magazines and newsagencies. In the field of science it keeps abreast of the times with several research laboratories and two observatories. To top it all, the Vatican is also a State—a small one, but nonetheless a State, complete with army and police, diplomatic corps, fire brigade, postal service, a mint, food and health services, and, of course, an administration.

The Church's missionaries, controlled by the Congregation of Propaganda Fide, are administered separately, as are all the religious orders: Benedictines, Dominicans, Franciscans, Augustinians, Carmelites, Jesuits and the rest, numbering a quarter of a million people in all. Added to these are the one million nuns divided among 1,300 orders. The various dioceses also have their own administrations, supervized by the Congregation for the Clergy. There are also several Roman Catholic foundations and institutes with separate funds, sources of income and budgets.

To keep track of all the activities connected with the Church of

Rome and of their financial implications would be a Herculean task too vast to undertake. I shall therefore mention, in order to give the reader some idea of the magnitude of the organization of the Catholic Church, three basic figures : about five million people (priests, monks, friars, nuns and lay persons, such as teachers, doctors and nurses) work for the Catholic Church; over twenty million boys and girls are educated in Catholic schools which range from kindergarten to university; and thirteen million adults and children receive assistance from Catholic charitable institutions.

This enquiry will concentrate on the core of the Pope's financial empire, that is on the offices and the men who control from Rome the properties, the funds and the investments depending directly upon the Holy See.

The secrecy surrounding this particular aspect of the financial system of the Catholic Church compelled the author to adopt the methods of a Nero Wolfe in view of the arm-chair character of the work of detection involved. At the beginning of my enquiry I had hoped that, after the Ecumenical Council and the advent of a modern-minded Pope like Paul VI, the cloak of financial secrecy could be lifted. But I was mistaken. My approaches to the usual information channels were fruitless. In all fairness I must say that my numerous Vatican contacts were all genuinely anxious to help. And when they in their turn met with a blank wall of denial, they were apologetic, embarrassed and frequently irritated to have to admit that Vatican finances were and must remain secret, at least for some time to come.

I then decided to take a short cut and to approach the Pope directly. The head of the *Osservatore Romano* press office, Dr Renato Casimirri, who is in constant touch with journalists and who, being a journalist himself, fully realizes the importance and advantages of frankness in public relations, suggested I should address my letter to the Pope's personal secretary, Mgr Pasquale Macchi. He, in daily contact with the Pope, living in the same apartment and sharing his devotions and meals, would surely see that my letter was read by Pope Paul personally. On the 26 June 1967, I therefore wrote :

Very Reverend Monsignore,

I am addressing myself to you, on the advice of Doctor Casimirri, with a request for help.

A German publisher has asked me to write a book on the finances of the Catholic Church and I have taken the pledge to do it. Other publishers in other countries have already shown a great interest in this book and I believe it may be published also in America, England, France and Italy, as it has happened with my two previous books dealing with the Vatican.

Some aspects of Vatican finances are known and fairly clear, others on the contrary are surrounded by a veil of mystery which breeds, rather than discourages, rumours and perhaps even legends about an alleged fabulous wealth of the Vatican.

I intend to write a truthful book, but in order to do this I need exact and first-hand information. I am sure that the Holy See has nothing to hide. Gone are the days (1870–80) when in the Parliaments and in the press it was suggested that the collection of Peter's Pence was disreputable.

Today, especially after the Council and after the *Populorum progressio*, the Church of Rome stands like the Church of the Poor. She also stands, without fear of denial, as the greatest welfare agency (*ente morale*) there ever was in the world dedicated to the spreading of education, culture, civilisation and peace and to relieve the sufferings and the misery of men. This image, however, is partially clouded and cheapened by that very aura of persistent and, in my opinion, useless secrecy which continues to surround certain aspects of Vatican finances.

I am certain that, if I could illustrate in my book, with official figures, the enormous financial burden the Church is compelled to sustain to carry out her mission and that if I could explain without reticence from whence the funds derive, I would do something useful to the cause of truth and to the Church herself.

I do not pretend to be able to publish a real and proper budget of the Catholic Church, as several Protestant Churches do. I am perfectly aware that the Church of Rome, with her centuries-old and complex traditions and structures, with the autonomous administrations of Propaganda Fide and the religious orders, etc., cannot too easily be constricted into a scheme. I have been told that nobody in the Vatican, and probably not even the Pope, has a complete picture of the financial situation. I have no hesitation in believing it. But I am equally certain that if the Holy Father would deign himself to authorise the Secretariat of State, the Administration of the Holy See Patrimony, the Special Administration, the Institute for Religious Works and the Governorship of the Vatican City State to supply me with authentic data, I could place my book on a solid and authoritative basis at least as far as the major financial organisations are concerned. Propaganda Fide, I am told, already publishes its income and expenditure and would not, therefore, represent a problem. And do you think I should include in my research the Congregation of the Council?[1]

As far as the historical part is concerned—Peter's Pence, the Apostolic Chamber, the Camerlengo, etc.—I am sufficiently well documented up to 1870. From then on there is a gap, at least regarding figures, and in this respect too I would need help.

I would like, to put it in short, to do a serious job: to take the main road instead of round-about ways and being compelled to collect rumours, confidential information, deductions and other approximate elements which would leave certain aspects of Vatican finances in an equivocal light. I would, therefore, be extremely grateful to you, Monsignore, if you would forward my request to the Holy Father whose love for truth encourages me to hope for a favourable reception.

On my part I take the pledge as from now to treat the matter with scruple, without sensationalism and to reproduce faithfully the data that may be supplied to me.

I never had any written answer to this letter. Instead, about a month later, the Italian Mgr Fausto Vallainc telephoned asking to see me. Mgr Vallainc was the official Vatican spokesman who held a press conference every Friday at which he answered, or did his best to answer, the many questions that Vatican correspondents put to him. He told me that my letter, of which he personally approved, had caused some stir in the Vatican, that it had been discussed at various levels and that opinions were divided. He himself thought that my request for authentic information should have been received favourably and that lifting the veil of secrecy would do more good than harm to the Church. He assured me he had expressed his favourable opinion in writing, but that the offices concerned with finances were very reserved and the final answer

[1] The name of which has since been changed into Congregation of the Clergy.

was therefore negative. Mgr Vallainc appeared genuinely sorry for the outcome of the affair. Anyhow, this was typical Vatican procedure. No direct answer, nothing put in writing, no indication of who exactly was responsible for the refusal.

In all fairness I must point out that my request for first-hand information came at a time when the Pope was planning to announce a general reform of the Roman Curia, including the sensitive area of finances. I understand that the Pope, who before being appointed Archbishop of Milan and before his election to the throne of Peter had spent thirty years in the State Secretariat and who therefore knew the Curia inside out, was dissatisfied with the running of finances. He had long intended to change things but had met with considerable opposition and passive resistance. Finally he took advantage of the general reform of the Curia to introduce a reform of Vatican finances along with it.

But what precisely is wrong with the Vatican finances? The criticism levelled against the way they are run at present is based on charges of nepotism (which touch neither Pope John nor Pope Paul personally, but go back to Pius XII), of absence of proper controls, of overlapping, of excessive power granted to a small group of Italian lay financiers, of the absence of a general financial policy, of a certain lack of foresight and, finally, of excessive and harmful secrecy. The very fact that Pope Paul has found it necessary to introduce a reform proves that present arrangements are not satisfactory.

Under the reform, which came into effect on 1 March 1968, a committee of three Cardinals was set up. They control, not all the financial activities of the Catholic Church (which would be too big a task and which is being done by other offices anyhow), but what one might call Vatican high finances, that is the administration of the property and funds directly owned by the Holy See and the big investments and financial transactions. The committee will also prepare a yearly budget to be submitted for the Pope's approval.

It is possible, but not yet certain, that this budget will be made public, once things have been put in order. This, as I pointed out in my letter to the Pope's secretary, is already the case with several Protestant Churches. Thus, the 1966/67 budget of the Church of England, for instance, amounted to £21,234,000 with an increase of 6.5 per cent over the previous year; that of the High Church of

Scotland was £8,860,643; and that of the Scottish Presbyterian Church of £650,000. The final decision on whether to follow the Protestant example will rest with the Pope. What seems unlikely is that official figures will be released before the new office, which has been rightly described as a kind of Budget Ministry, has had time to establish itself, hire the necessary personnel, take stock of the situation and organize its own accounts. Things move very slowly in the Vatican and it is generally expected that three or four years, if not more, will elapse before publication of the first official budget of the Holy See. Even then it might only be read privately by the Pope.

In the meantime all one can do is try to unravel the mystery of Vatican finances through detective work. At first glance, nothing would seem to be less secret than the financing of the Holy See. All the various Vatican offices that deal with financial matters are clearly defined in their functions and jurisdictions by the Code of Canon Law or by Papal documents; moreover the Pontifical Year-book carefully lists all these offices together with their telephone numbers and the names of people employed, from the Cardinals at the top down to the most humble lay accountants and typists. In other words, everything is known, open and official—except for one important thing: the actual amount of money involved.

This book, therefore, will have to move on two entirely different types of ground. Solid so far as the structure and the scope of Vatican financial administrations are concerned; and marshy when attempting a precise assessment of the present wealth of the Holy See. The work of detection I mentioned earlier therefore concerns only the marshy ground. I have used many different sources: information of a confidential nature gathered from Vatican officials; information from Italian and international banking quarters that are linked to the Vatican; previous writings on the subject gathered and collated from books, magazines, newspapers and agencies; and of course logical deductions to be drawn from official documents and pronouncements.

The final result, in view of the Vatican refusal to let exact figures be known, is not entirely satisfactory. I only hope that, by displaying a sense of proportion and of discrimination, by not taking too seriously the fabulous accounts about the colossal wealth of the Church put out by Communist and other anti-clerical sources, by not completely trusting the attempts of Catholic apologists to minimize the same, by relying a bit more on the estimates of sober, level-headed bankers and businessmen who are in touch with Vatican administrations, I have succeeded in getting fairly near the truth.

1

Give Unto Caesar

'Thou shalt not lend upon usury to thy
brother; usury of money, usury of victuals,
usury of any thing that is lent upon usury:
Unto a stranger thou mayest lend upon
usury; but unto thy brother thou shalt not
lend upon usury: that the LORD thy God
may bless thee in all that thou settest thine
hand to in the land whither thou goest to
possess it.'

Deuteronomy 23: 19-20

Until the Protestant Reformation, and, to a lesser extent, right up
until our own time, the above quotation has deeply influenced not
only the tragic history of the Jewish people but that of the Catholic
Church and of Western civilization in general.

The two sentences it contains have been the cause of heated and
learned disputes lasting for centuries, and of continuous moral
embarrassment and doubt for both Christians and Jews. The key
words are 'brother' and 'stranger' (*ahika* and *nokri* in Hebrew). To
begin with, the general opinion was that 'brother' should not be
taken in a restrictive, familiar sense, but stood for all the members
of the Jewish tribes and all the followers of the Jewish creed, and
that 'stranger' meant everybody else. St Jerome, in the Vulgate,
translated *nokri* as *alienus*. In other words, Jews were not allowed
to lend money or other goods or services to other Jews, but were
allowed and even encouraged to do so to non-Jews. It was all
rather simple.

The real trouble started when Christianity, which looked upon
the Old Testament as divine revelation, became the official religion
of the whole Roman Empire. Who was then to be considered a
brother and who a stranger? In view of the Christian conception
that all men were brothers and of the universal spirit that animated

14

the Church of Rome, the tendency was to condemn the lending out of money at interest as a sin in itself. There was no clear distinction between lending money at exorbitant rates and at reasonable rates of interest. It was all usury.

Civil law, especially in the Carolingian era, often based itself upon Christian morals, and usury was strictly forbidden to ecclesiastics and laymen alike. Only Jews were allowed to become moneylenders. Thus was born a widespread hostility against the Jews, from which stemmed the character of Shylock, the ghettos, the pogroms and finally Hitler's hallucinating 'ultimate solution'.

Christians were affected by Deuteronomy almost as much as the Jews. The old taboo, continuously violated or circumvented by ingenious tricks, was still present and it acted as a brake against an economic system based on credit and against the development of an industrial economy in the modern sense of the word. Among the various tricks employed was the so-called 'mohatra contract', devised by Jesuits, whereby if a man was short of ready cash, he could buy from a merchant goods worth, say, 100 francs and undertake to pay in a year's time. On the same day he would resell to the same merchant the same goods for 80 francs in cash. The undertaking to pay 100 francs in a year's time still stood. Thus, by a fictitious purchase and an equally fictitious sale of goods, the person in question had borrowed money at 20 per cent interest.

The German Protestant Reformation represented a turning point in the history of the interpretation of Deuteronomy. In those days of profound social upheavals two opposing schools of thought existed. There were those who preached that interest, usury and even the acquisition of private property were against the teachings of both Moses and Christ. In the New Jerusalem, according to these preachers, all men were to be brothers who lived in a spirit of mutual love without exploiting each other. But the more sedate reformers, like Luther, Melanton, Swingli, Bucerus, saw in these theories an incitement to revolution and the danger of complete anarchy. Rather than face that danger they proclaimed that the law of Moses was dead and that the New Testament should not serve as the basis for civil laws. While they did not advocate usury in its worst form, they encouraged the lending and borrowing of money at fair interest rates, thus preparing the ground for the advent of capitalism.

For capitalism was unable to accept the dicta of Deuteronomy. The outright condemnation of any form of usury would have severely restricted economic activities and prevented the accumulation of capital. The discrimination against foreigners, on the other hand, supposed a state of perennial warfare, or at least hostility, which would have jeopardized stability and international trade relations. Calvin devised a brilliant, if somewhat specious, way around the dilemma. He invalidated the discrimination against foreigners by appealing to universal Christian brotherhood and he cancelled the prohibition of usury by quoting the exception made by the Bible itself.

In the Catholic world the process of demolition of Deuteronomy was much slower. Although by the middle of the eighteenth century some Catholic jurists had seriously undermined it, it went on leading a spectral existence in the more traditionalist quarters almost until our day. The Protestant approach to economy was at the basis of the development of modern capitalism and of the spectacular progress achieved in modern times by the Anglo-Saxon Protestant countries (Germany, England, Scandinavia, USA, Canada, Australia), as compared with the slower development of the Catholic countries (Italy, Spain, Portugal, Latin America). It was therefore up to the Catholic Church to change its attitude towards money, private property, credit and other financial problems.

Christ himself based his preaching and his entire conception of life on the assumption that the Kingdom of God was near. 'But I tell you of a truth, there be some standing here, which shall not taste of death, till they see the kingdom of God.' (Luke 9: 27.) Everything was projected either in a life after death or in an imminent Golden Age in which all the peoples of the earth would recognize the only true God and his justice would reign.

Contemporary life was for Christ a mere transitory phase and it was therefore natural that he should not attach any value to worldly goods. He himself came from a poor family and chose all the apostles from among poor people. Christ not only chased the merchants and the moneychangers from the temple but issued the terrible warning that it would have been 'easier for a camel to go through a needle's eye, than for a rich man to enter into the kingdom of God.' (Luke 18: 25.)

His whole attitude was against money, wealth and against saving, as he didn't believe in making provisions for future necessities. Divine providence would somehow take care of everything. 'Consider the ravens : for they neither sow nor reap; which neither have storehouse nor barn; and God feedeth them : how much are ye better than the fowls? Consider the lilies how they grow : they toil not, they spin not; and yet I say unto you, that Solomon in all his glory was not arrayed like one of these.' (Luke 12: 24, 27.)

Nor does one find in the New Testament any particular appreciation of the moral value of work, as the episode of Martha and Mary in Bethany indicates. It was, with all due respect, a position very similar to that of the present day beatniks, dropouts, hippies or flower children.

There are, of course, many other points of contact between Christ's teachings and the conception and mode of life of the hippy or the beatnik : pacifism, a disregard for conventions and for the Establishment, scant attachment to family bonds and the substitution of family life by 'group' life, and even an unconventional mode of dressing.

Christ himself disregarded the Sabbath and made fun of those who observed it. As for his attitude towards his own family, and to family ties in general, there are several significant episodes and sayings. He was once in a house telling one of his parables when he was informed that his mother and brothers were outside, that they couldn't get in because of the crowd and wanted to see him. He replied : 'My mother and my brethren are these which hear the word of God, and do it.' (Luke 8: 21.) On another occasion, 'a certain woman of the company lifted up her voice and said unto him, Blessed is the womb that bare thee, and the paps which thou hast sucked. But he said, Yea rather, blessed are they that hear the word of God and keep it.' (Luke 11: 27-8.) Christ told a man to follow him and hearing the man reply : 'Lord, suffer me first to go and bury my father', Christ answered, 'Let the dead bury their dead.' (Luke 9: 59-60.)

As for the possession of worldly goods, he instructed his disciples : 'Take nothing for your journey, neither staves, nor scrip, neither bread, neither money; neither have two coats apiece.' (Luke 9: 3.) And on another occasion he forbade them to wear shoes.

But here the similarities[1] between the followers of Christ and the young boys and girls who today let their hair grow, go barefoot and wear the badge : 'Make Love, Not War' end. Christ and his disciples were out to 'catch men', to save as many souls as possible from eternal damnation, and to spread a supernatural message. The beatniks and hippies, at least until they find their own prophet, seem to be motivated by a curious blend of impulses in which spiritual values, an attraction towards oriental mysticism, pure laziness, political ideals, irresponsibility, a spirit of reform, a spirit of contradiction at all costs, exhibitionism, the easy satisfaction of sexual urges and, alas, the use of drugs combine.

The parallel between the first Christians and the hippies was drawn from a purely economic viewpoint. To show by taking an example how difficult it would be today, and was then, to organize a society which would abolish the motivations of bettering one's standard of living, acquiring possessions and a sense of security, and providing for the future of one's children.

The early Christians more or less conformed to the pattern of life laid down by Christ and the Apostles. They were mostly slaves, labourers, artisans—people of humble extraction for whom poverty was a natural condition. There were also a few members of the middle class and of the aristocracy who were converted to the new creed and gave up their worldly possessions. But they were exceptions.

As the Christian religion became an official state religion, and when the Bishop of Rome became not only a spiritual but also a temporal ruler, it was inevitable that Christ's teaching should be interpreted to meet practical and actual circumstances, something that could happen in a lifetime. This applied not only to the Catholic Church after it had acquired temporal power but also to those empires, kingdoms, communes and republics that professed Christianity. The original dichotomy, the contrast between what was divinely desirable (poverty, charity, unselfishness, relying on providence) and what was humanly possible, the blending of the spiritual with the temporal, persists to the present time.

The solution to this dichotomy depends heavily on a single sentence by Christ : 'Render therefore unto Caesar the things which

[1] The late Californian Bishop James Pike also noted the similarity and added: 'There is something about the temper and quality of these people, a gentleness, an interest—something good.'

are Caesar's; and unto God the things that are God's.' (Matthew 22: 21.)

It was pronounced by Christ, as we know, in answer to a deliberately tricky question posed to him by one of his enemies. Were his followers supposed to pay taxes or not? Had he answered 'no', as the general trend of his preaching led one to suppose, this could have been interpreted as an act of rebellion against the Roman rule and would have led to his arrest and possible death sentence. The Pharisees would have been rid of this troublesome and embarrassing prophet without having to assume any direct responsibility. But Jesus asked to be shown a coin and, having pointed out that it bore the image of the Roman Emperor, pronounced the famous phrase.

Christ's recommendation has been twisted and stretched to justify not only the imposition and the exaction of taxes, but also compulsory conscription, military discipline, warfare, sentencing of conscientious objectors, the death penalty, and the enforcement of penal and civil laws—in short, all those measures that are deemed necessary for the orderly development, and sometimes for the survival, of a society. Ironically, it was also later used to assert the complete separation of Church from State, to proclaim the independence of civil authorities from ecclesiastical rule and to justify the termination of papal temporal power.

During the centuries in which Christ's representative on earth was also a Caesar, the Church's attitude to political economy did not (and objectively could not) differ too much, at least in practice, from that of the other States with which she had to compete on a temporal basis. The apogee of papal temporal power was reached under the reign of Innocent III (1198–1216) who interfered with the affairs of Germany, making and un-making emperors, and who compelled Philip Augustus of France, Peter of Aragon, Alfonso IX of Spain, Sancho of Portugal, Ladislaus of Poland and John of England to bow to his iron will. The supremacy of the Roman Church over all civil authorities found a definite formulation in the bull by Boniface VIII, *Unam Sanctam* (1302) which proclaimed that the source of all temporal power was spiritual power, that is in substance the Pope himself. 'We therefore declare, affirm, define and pronounce that to be subjected to the Roman Pontiff is an absolutely necessary condition for every human being, for his salvation.' But things had changed since Innocent III and the European kingdoms, having asserted themselves as strong national units, were not disposed to let themselves be ruled by a foreign power. Already his successor Benedict XI had to moderate the intransigence shown by Boniface against France, while the next Pope, Clement V (1305–14), was elected in France, became practically a vassal of the French monarchy and inaugurated the so-called Avignon captivity.

It is evident that by exercising temporal power with such intensity and conviction, the Pope being in effect an absolute monarch, the bishops feudal lords and a large proportion of the clergy in the Papal States holding key posts in the administrative machinery—the Church of Rome came, almost inevitably, to identify herself with the interests of the ruling class and of the Establishment. If not from the doctrinal point of view, she became in practice conservative and often reactionary.

The French Revolution (whose more violent supporters promised to 'strangle the last king with the entrails of the last priest') shocked the Church of Rome, in a way understandably, into an even more marked support of absolutism and conservation. All new ideas— from liberalism to socialism, from the birth of the trade unions to Italy's urge for national independence and unity, from Darwinism to Malthusianism—practically anything that could change or threaten the established order, were bitterly opposed and condemned by Rome. The climax of conservatism and reaction was reached in the *Syllabus* (1864), a long list of contemporary philosophies, trends, political and economic ideas and movements to be condemned, by Pius IX, a Pope who had started as a liberal and a patriot and ended exactly the opposite.

But the Church of Rome could not sit for ever condemning, rejecting, threatening, excommunicating and going against the times. She could not ignore for ever the great economic, technological, social and political upheavals that had been and still are changing the face not only of Western civilization but of the whole world. She could not, because of the very Christian spirit on which she was founded, keep siding with the strong against the weak, with the exploiters against the exploited. The change was a slow and painful process, but it did take place.

The first, or rather the most outspoken change in the ideological course of the bark of Peter was the encyclical *Rerum novarum* issued by Leo XIII in 1891, twenty-one years after Pius IX had been deprived of temporal power. In it the Church of Rome at last took notice of the appalling conditions to which industrial workers were reduced and suggested remedies. Leo XIII wrote as an introduction :

> The ardent hunger for novelty which started a long time ago to agitate the people, was bound to pass as a matter of course from the political order to the similar order of social economy. In fact the portentous progress of the arts [today we would call it 'technology'] and of the new methods of industry; the changed relations between masters and workers; the fact that wealth has accumulated in a few hands and poverty has become widespread; the feeling of their force which in the working classes has become more lively and their unity closer; all these things, with the addition of a deterioration of customs, have caused the conflict to explode. . . . It is a difficult and dangerous question. Difficult, because it is very arduous to define precise boundaries in the relations between the owners and the proletariat, between capital and labour. Dangerous, because turbulent and astute men are everywhere endeavouring to distort judgment and to exploit the issue to perturb the people.

It was, as one can easily detect from the tone, not an eager but a rather grudging acceptance of the 'novelty', partially attributed to the 'deterioration of customs'. But at least it meant facing realities. Leo's encyclical went much further and, besides analysing the illness, it also suggested remedies.

The *Rerum novarum* adds :

> It is clear, and everybody agrees on this, that it is extremely necessary to come to the help, without delay and with adequate provisions, of the proletarians, who as a whole find themselves in very miserable conditions, unworthy of man. For, the corporations of arts and trades having been suppressed in the last century and not replaced by anything else, and as the institutions and laws have moved away from the Christian spirit, it has happened that little by little the workers have become isolated and undefended both against the greed of

the owners and against unbridled competition. The disease was spread by a devouring usury which, although so many times condemned by the Church, goes on all the same, under other aspects, because of greedy speculators. To this one must add the monopoly of production and commerce, so that a very small number of ultra-rich have imposed on an infinite multitude of proletarians a yoke nearly akin to slavery.

It could be Proudhon, Engels or Marx speaking. Or the principles of early Christianity coming to life again. The encyclical continues :

The fortunate ones of our century are warned that riches do not free them from suffering and that they are damaging, rather than helping, future happiness; that the rich must tremble thinking of the extraordinarily severe threats of Jesus Christ; that one day they will have to give a very rigorous account of the use of their riches to God the judge.

Leo XIII goes a long way in urging the Governments to intervene in favour of the proletariat and to try to prevent strikes by abolishing the causes of strikes, in admitting the right of the workers to form trade unions (unless they be led by atheists) and, on the whole, displays an open and progressive attitude towards the problem.

All the improvements in the workers' conditions, however, are seen as concessions from above, either spontaneously granted by the owners themselves or enforced by the State, as duties to be performed in application of Christian charity. They are not yet seen as rights the workers are entitled to fight for and there is also a long passage in praise of 'the advantages of poverty' which, of course, encouraged resignation. Above all, and this is what interests us more from the economic point of view, the encyclical contains a determined stand in favour of private property and an equally strong condemnation of socialism. After having stated that private property 'conforms to the law of nature . . . (and is) confirmed by human and divine law', the encyclical adds :

The communion of goods suggested by socialism must be entirely rejected, because it harms those whom it wants to benefit, it offends the natural right of all, it alters the functions of the State and disturbs the peace.

But it is useful to consider carefully some details of major importance. The foremost is this : the Governments, through wise laws, must assure private property. One must keep the plebeians in harness, especially today, when so many uncontrolled desires are rampant. While justice permits the plebeians to try and better their condition, neither justice nor common good allow them to damage other people's property nor, under the pretext of I don't know what equality, to invade what belongs to somebody else. . . . Let the authority of the State intervene and when the trouble-makers have been harnessed, let it preserve the good workers from being seduced and the legitimate masters from being despoiled.

The paternalistic and authoritarian tone of the encyclical needs no comment.

Eighty-six years later, in March 1967, another fundamental and explosive social encyclical was issued by Paul VI, *Populorum progressio*. The ground for this document, which synthesises the position of the Church of Rome towards the most burning problems of our day after the Ecumenical Council, was prepared by the encyclicals *Mater et magistra* and *Pacem in terris* by Pope John. We shall not deal at length with Pope John's two masterly encyclicals because they are to a great extent embodied or brought a step forward by the *Populorum progressio*. There is, however, a passage in the *Pacem in terris* which has a decisive bearing on the attitude of the Catholic Church towards politics and economics—so often the same thing. In his all-embracing love for humanity, Pope John wrote :

One must never confuse error and the person who errs, not even when there is question of error or inadequate knowledge of truth in the moral or religious field. The person who errs is always and above all a human being, and he retains in every case his dignity as a human person; and he must always be regarded and treated in accordance with that lofty dignity.

He then extended this benign and optimistic conception of human nature to the much wider field of politics :

It must be borne in mind, furthermore, that neither can false philosophical teachings regarding the nature, origin and destiny

of the universe and of man, be identified with historical movements that have economic, social, cultural or political ends,
not even when these movements have originated from those
teachings and have drawn and still draw inspiration therefrom.
Because the teachings, once they are drawn up and defined,
remain always the same, while the movements, working on
historical situations in constant evolution, cannot but be
influenced by the latter and cannot avoid, therefore, being
subject to changes, even of a profound nature. Besides, who
can deny that those movements, in so far as they conform to
the dictates of right reason and are interpreters of the lawful
aspirations of the human person, contain elements that are
positive and deserving of approval?

The distinction made by Pope John between philosophical ideas
and the political movements or parties based on them, has a
fundamental importance. Liberalism, socialism, materialism and
more specifically Marxism have been strongly condemned by the
Catholic Church. But such ideas have given rise to political parties
which have gone through a considerable evolution. For instance,
the Italian Liberals, who in the days of Roncalli's youth were rabid
anti-clericals, advocating the confiscation of Church property and
the closing down of Catholic schools, have today become practically
allies of the Church. They are more conservative than the British
Conservative Party, and they defend private schools (the majority
of which are Catholic) on the principle of the freedom of teaching.

The larger part of the British Labour Party, which started out
on materialistic, class-struggle, Marxist assumptions, has turned to
a moderate, enlightened socialism which Italian Catholics take as
an example worth following. The same applies in different degrees
to socialism in West Germany, Austria, Scandinavia, Belgium, Italy
and many other countries.

What Pope John meant was that, although liberalism and
socialism were originally based on wrong philosophical premises, at
least from the Catholic doctrinal point of view, they have evolved,
and they both now contain some good of which the Catholic
Church can approve and even encourage; liberalism upholds freedom and the dignity of the human being; socialism is permeated
by ideas of social justice and solidarity which formed a great part
of Christ's teaching.

One can even envisage the day when, should communism give up persecuting religion and embark on the road of liberalisation of both politics and economy, a road along which Marshal Tito is already cautiously moving, and should the experiment fan out successfully, the Church of Rome will have nothing to object to in such regimes, even if they should continue to call themselves communist.

But let us return to the *Populorum progressio*, a document which was strongly influenced by the thought of the progressive wing of French Catholicism, including Cardinal Garrone, who worked on it with the Pope, the theologians Fathers L. J. Lebret, M. D. Chenu, H. de Lubac and, last but not least, the lay Catholic writer Jacques Maritain. The spirit that animates it all is definitely socialist, at least as far as economic theories are concerned.

The encyclical ranges over a large number of subjects, from peace to the United Nations, from the population explosion to the assistance to be given to underdeveloped countries, from the missions to education, from emigration to racial tensions. We shall examine only a few points that are more closely connected with economy.

Although, as is always the case with the Roman Church, the pretence is kept up that the fundamental doctrine never changes and although we find in the *Populorum progressio* one reference to the *Rerum novarum* and three to other documents by Leo XIII, an abyss separates the two encyclicals.

First of all the conception of private property as an absolute right sanctioned by divine, natural and human laws, which Leo XIII had so firmly stated, was reversed by Pope Paul. In this respect the *Populorum progressio* reads:

> The recent Council has recalled that 'God has destined the earth and all it contains for the use of all men and of all peoples, so that the goods of creation must flow in just proportion into the hands of everybody, according to the rule of justice which is inseparable from charity.' All other rights, of whatever kind, including those of private property and of free trade, must be subordinated to it: they must not obstruct, but on the contrary foster its achievement, and it is a grave and urgent social duty to restore them to their original aims.

Pope Paul quoted a passage from St Ambrose: 'You never give to the poor what is yours: you merely return to them what belongs to them. For what you have appropriated was given for the common use of everybody. The land is given to everybody, and not only to the rich.'

He then added his own comment: 'It is the same as saying that private property does not constitute for anybody an unconditional and absolute right. Nobody is authorized to keep for his exclusive use what exceeds his needs, when others are lacking the means of livelihood. . . . The common good occasionally requires the expropriation of certain estates which constitute an obstacle to common prosperity because of their vastness, or because they are not sufficiently cultivated or because they considerably damage the interests of the country.'

There is no mention in Pope Paul's encyclical of the necessity on the part of the State 'to keep the plebeians in harness' which Leo XIII had urged. On the contrary, we find the following passage:

> There certainly are situations where injustice cries to heaven. When entire populations, lacking the means of livelihood, live in such a state of dependence that they are excluded from any initiative and responsibility, and from any possibility of cultural promotion and of taking part in social and political life, there is a great temptation to resist with violence these insults to human dignity. However, we know a revolutionary insurrection—except in the case of an evident and prolonged tyranny which seriously violates the fundamental rights of the person and which damages in a dangerous way the common good of the country—is a source of fresh injustice, introduces a new unbalance and causes further destruction. One cannot fight a real evil at the cost of a greater evil.

Even if only with many reservations, Paul VI has thus recognized, exceptionally, the right of the people to revolt against the Establishment, if such an Establishment has turned into a ruthless and harmful dictatorship. The whole idea, however, has been left extremely vague. And so has been the criterion by which to decide what is an 'evident and prolonged' tyranny, what 'seriously violates' the fundamental rights of the person and what damages 'in a dangerous way' the common good. Does Mao's 'cultural' revolution qualify for an uprising? Has the Russian regime sufficiently violated the fundamental human rights? Have the dictatorships of Franco and Salazar been evident, prolonged and harmful enough to justify insurrection? And what about Nasser, Boumedienne, the Greek generals and the various dictators of Latin America and post-colonial Africa? And must one put up with tyrannies if they violate the fundamental right of the person, but not 'seriously', or damage the common good, but not 'dangerously'?

It would be useless, in view of the tradition of the Popes to couch all their pronouncements in general, abstract and often Lapalissian terms, to expect any clear-cut answer to these questions. What matters is that some sort of exception to the general rule of resignation and non-violence has been made and that revolutionary movements may find, or hope they will find, the Church of Rome at their side.

Another highlight of the *Populorum progressio* is a violent, almost virulent attack on 'liberal capitalism' which involves also some of the pillars of what is loosely known as the American way of life. Pope Paul wrote:

> Industrialization, being necessary to economic growth and to human progress, is both a symptom and a factor of development. . . . But unfortunately under these new conditions of society a system was instituted which considered profit as an essential factor of economic progress, competition as the supreme law of economy, and private possession of the means of production as an absolute right, without limits or corresponding social duties. This unbridled liberalism led to a dictatorship, which was rightly denounced by Pius XI as the origin of 'the international imperialism of money'. One can never condemn sufficiently similar abuses, while once again solemnly recalling that economy is at the service of man. But if it is true that a certain capitalism was the source of so many sufferings, of so many injustices and fratricidal wars, the effects of which still continue, it would be wrong to attribute to industrialization itself the ills which are due to the nefarious system that accompanied it. On the contrary and to pay homage to justice, one must recognize the irreplaceable contribution made by the organization of work and by industrial progress to economic development.

The supporters of capitalism have remarked in this respect that without the powerful incentive of profit, without the accumulation of capital guaranteed by private property and the equally powerful stimulus of free competition, Western civilization would never have achieved the spectacular prosperity and technological expertise which enabled it to help the underdeveloped countries and to fight hunger, poverty and disease all over the world. They also noted that the USA, where the tenets condemned by the Pope have found the most vigorous expression, has done more in this respect than any other country and that her powerful industrial potential—born out of liberal capitalism and based on it—has materially contributed to the freeing of Europe from Nazism, and in containing the spread of atheistic communism. They furthermore noted that Russia, her satellites and Yugoslavia are re-introducing the elements of profit and competition, and to a lesser extent of private property, in an attempt to stimulate their unliberal, cumbersome and slow-moving economies.

The controversy about political economy is not within our scope —which is only that of outlining what the Church of Rome, through the words of her supreme representative, thinks today about these problems after the findings of the Ecumenical Council. Keeping within these limits one should note that the main concern of the *Populorum progressio*, as the opening words of the encyclical indicate, is the moral duty, and also in the long run the interest, of the prosperous countries to help the underdeveloped countries towards an acceptable standard of living.

Pope Paul, besides touching many aspects of the problem, also denounced as a big obstacle the workings of international trade. I shall try to condense as much as possible a long argument he developed in the encyclical and which is fundamentally shared by the Food and Agriculture Organisation of the United Nations. The highly industrialized countries, the Pope wrote, do in fact help the developing countries with sometimes considerable financial and technical aid. But the effectiveness of this aid is practically annulled by the fact that the rich, industrialized countries sell to the poorer countries mostly manufactured goods and buy from them mostly agricultural products and raw materials. 'But while the manufactured goods, thanks to technological progress, increase in value rapidly and find ready markets, the raw materials coming from the developing countries are subjected to drastic and sudden variations in prices which do not keep up with the progressive increase in value of the manufactured goods.' The result of all this, according to Pope Paul, is that the developing countries cannot rely on their exports of agricultural and raw materials to finance their plans of development. 'In the end the poor always remain poor and the rich become even richer.'

Pope Paul, again, placed all the blame on liberalism :

> One must face it, it is the fundamental principle of liberalism as a rule for commercial trading that is being questioned. . . . An economy of exchange cannot be based exclusively on the law of free competition which only too often generates an economic dictatorship. Freedom of exchange is not fair unless it is subordinated to the necessities of social justice.

The Pope then remarked that the developed countries already take into account this necessity in their own economies, and in their relations with other developed countries, by either subsidizing agriculture at the expense of industry, or by protecting it by special fiscal and financial measures applied within the frames of the common markets. He would like to see the same principles and practices extended also to the developing countries.

'One must not and one does not wish to suggest the abolition of a market based on competition.' The Pope explains, 'What we mean is that one should keep competition within certain limits that would make it just and moral, and therefore human. In the trade between developed and developing countries, the starting points are too far apart and the actual freedom of action is too unequally distributed. Social justice commands that international trade, if it wants to be something human and moral, should re-establish among the parties at least a relative equality of chances. The latter can only be a long-term objective. But to reach it one should as from now create a real equality in the discussions and the negotiations.'

To sum up, the Catholic Church's present conception of political economy, as outlined in the latest papal document, is a kind of mild democratic socialism, based not on class struggle but rather on the Christian principles of charity, justice and respect for the individual. It also shows a deep mistrust of capitalism and the liberal conception of economy. The ancient ghost of Deuteronomy still seems to hover in the background.

2

Peter's Pence

> 'We have no riches belonging to Us, but to
> Us are entrusted the custody and the dis-
> tribution of the substance of the poor.'
>
> St Gregory the Great

One of the main sources of income of the Holy See, and one which
in certain periods was practically the only one, is Peter's Pence.

As a regular, organized way of collecting money, Peter's Pence
has an Anglo-Saxon origin. One must go back to St Gregory the
Great (590–604) under whose pontificate and direction St Augustine
of Canterbury was sent to England with the mission of converting
the Angles to Christianity. After the conversion many Englishmen
acquired the habit of making a pilgrimage to Rome. Also King
Caedwalla, as the Venerable Bede related, came to Rome to have
'the special glory' of receiving baptism and dying there.

His successor, King Ina (689–726) abdicated after reigning for
thirty-seven years to go to die in Rome. The number of English
pilgrims gradually increased and by the end of the eighth century
a kind of pilgrims' home was founded and called Schola Saxonum.
It was located in a district close to St Peter's, which became known
as Burgus Saxonum, and which to this very day is called Borgo.

This home for the pilgrims was founded by King Ina or, according to other sources, by Offa II. In order to give the English
pilgrims in Rome financial help, King Ina enforced a yearly tax
of one penny on every family living in the kingdom of Wessex.
Peter's Pence was officially born.

The tax became known as Romscot, that is the scot to be paid
to Rome. It was confirmed by Offa II, King of Mercia, and placed
on a regular basis by King Ethelwulf. This king used to send to
Rome annually the sum of three hundred mangons which were

thus divided : one hundred to buy the oil for the lamps in St Peter's basilica; one hundred for the oil used in the basilica of St Paul; and one hundred for the personal use of the 'universal apostolic Pope'.

The habit of collecting money for the Church of Rome gradually spread to other countries. Charlemagne extended it to France and his empire and· made the levy compulsory for all the owners of houses and land. He was thus able to collect 1,200 lire annually. Canute (1014–33) introduced it to Denmark. When the Normans occupied the Two Sicilies (1059) they immediately started collecting Peter's Pence to underline the end of the Arab domination and the return to Christianity.

The English cardinal Nicholas Breakspeare, who was to become Pope Hadrian IV, brought the custom to Norway when he was Papal Legate there (1148–54). It was introduced in Spain in 1073, in Bohemia in 1075, in Croatia and Dalmatia in 1076, in Portugal in 1144. It also extended to Poland, Ukraine and the Catholic Orient.

It is not in fact easy to distinguish between spontaneous offerings by the faithful, taxes levied by local rulers and sent to Rome and feudal taxes paid to the Pope in exchange for his protection. Of this we shall speak later when dealing with the Apostolic Chamber.

The history of Peter's Pence was inevitably connected with the political and religious storms the Church of Rome had to face throughout the centuries. In England the collection of Peter's Pence was abolished by Henry VIII in 1534 when he proclaimed himself head of the Church of England, was re-established by Queen Mary and definitely suppressed by Queen Elizabeth in 1558, at least as a tax. The Protestant Reform and the Anglican secession dealt a hard blow to Vatican finances not only because the collection of Peter's Pence, and of feudal and ecclesiastical tributes stopped in the countries concerned, but also because the properties of the Catholic Church were often confiscated. After the Reformation one could say that, broadly speaking, the main source of income for the Holy See was the taxes levied on the Papal Domains.

Peter's Pence, in the present meaning of the word, that is as an entirely voluntary contribution by the faithful, was reborn in the middle of the nineteenth century out of the Pope's misfortunes. When the Roman Republic was proclaimed in 1848 and Pope

Pius IX was forced to flee to the city-fortress of Gaeta, Catholics all over the world were deeply moved. This feeling was voiced in Paris by Count Charles de Montalembert who in a speech to the Chamber of Peers in 1849 exclaimed : 'Since Catholic France has not had the honour to welcome the Pope in exile, should it not at least show by its deeds that it shares in his trials?' These words were followed by action. A committee was formed in Paris to collect the *Denier de Saint-Pierre* and bishops all over the world were invited to help the Pope through collections gathered in the various dioceses. De Montalembert's committee branched out first to Turin and then to Vienna where, in 1860, a confraternity named after St Michael began to operate for this purpose. The confraternity spread to Ireland and then to the whole of Europe, North and South America and the mission lands. There were many similar committees. The Catholics of Gand set up a special office to collect donations and a booklet written by Monsignor de Ségur to incite Catholics to help the Pope financially sold no less than 100,000 copies, a best-seller for those days.

The Vatican, to which the Pope had returned, set up a special office to administer the funds that had started pouring in from all over the world. Two briefs, issued respectively on 31 October and 4 November 1860, established the confraternities of St Peter which had the task of 'aiding the Holy See'. A Confrérie de Saint-Pierre was also formed in France and the Tournai branch particularly distinguished itself.

On 20 September 1870, the plumed Bersaglieri of the Piedmontese general Cadorna stormed through the breach of Porta Pia, occupied Rome and put an end to the temporal power of the Pope. The main source of income of the Holy See—the taxes, the excises, and the customs collected from the Papal States—was thus totally extinguished. It was then that Peter's Pence saved the Holy See from total bankruptcy.

In many European countries, and particularly in Germany and Ireland, the parish priests would distribute to the faithful picture-cards depicting the Pope lying on a bed of straw in a dark dungeon to corroborate the legend that he was a prisoner of the wicked Italians and reduced to extreme poverty. It was, of course, a symbolic picture, but many humble people took it literally and pfennigs, pennies, shillings, ducats, thalers, pengoes and dollars poured in, to constitute the main revenue of the Holy See.

The collection of funds often took some rather naïve and moving forms, like the Pious Society which was formed among the poorest classes of Naples and which was called the 'Waste Paper and Needlework Society for Aid to the Holy Father'. In 1874 the First Italian Catholic Congress was held in Venice, which later gave rise to the central office for the organization of congresses and prepared the way for the foundation of Catholic Action as it is today. During this congress the Catholic Youth organization announced proudly that it had collected 1,714,061 lire for Peter's Pence, which for those days was quite a considerable sum.

Anti-clericalism was rampant at the time, particularly in Italy which had been for too long under the despotic and inept temporal rule of the Popes and which had seen in the Papacy a big obstacle to national unity. Pious societies were disbanded, seminaries and colleges closed down and ecclesiastic property confiscated. Attempts were made in the Italian parliament between 1870 and 1880 to outlaw the collection of Peter's Pence and in certain cases the police actually interfered. In 1866 the *Osservatore Cattolico* stopped publishing the names of contributors to Peter's Pence for fear they might get into trouble with the authorities. Similar reactions were to be found in other countries. One only has to recall Bismark's Kulturkampf and note that, as late as 1917, the Belgian paper *Le Siécle XX* suggested to the government that Peter's Pence should be stopped.

It is probably because of the hostility which civil authorities manifested against the Church and because of the inherent danger in those days of disclosing sources and figures of income, that the Vatican has adopted the rule of surrounding all financial affairs by top secrecy. The natural Vatican caution and reserve has done the rest and the secrecy, as we saw, has been maintained to the present day, breeding the legend of a fantastic wealth belonging to the Holy See and of the Pope as a big financier, as depicted in Hochhuth's play *The Deputy*.

Today Peter's Pence is organized in the following way. Every year on a certain day in all the Catholic churches in the world a collection is held for the Pope. Generally the day is 29 June, Saint Peter's day, but in many dioceses it is done on another day, preferably a Sunday, more suitable for the faithful and likely to bring in more cash. In Italy the money is collected by the bishops and sent to the Secretariat of State in Rome. In other countries it is given to the nuncios, internuncios or apostolic delegates who in turn send it to the State Secretariat. On less frequent occasions, when the collection happens to coincide with a visit to Rome by a cardinal or a bishop, Peter's Pence is handed directly to the Pope in the form of a cheque.

Naturally the contributions to Peter's Pence from each diocese vary enormously according to its size, the wealth and the religious zeal of its inhabitants, the efficiency of its clergy, and the nature of local tradition. While some of the smallest and poorest Italian dioceses contribute only a few hundred thousand lire, United States Cardinals and bishops are known to have sent or brought to the Pope at times sums in the region of $\frac{1}{2}$ million or more. The United States is the biggest contributor to Peter's Pence.

Not all the money in this fund is collected in churches or religious institutions on an appointed day. Letters from individuals pour in daily addressed to the Pope personally, or to the Holy See or the State Secretariat in general, containing large cheques or more frequently small banknotes. This money is turned over to the State Secretariat and added to the fund. As we shall see later, it is possible, despite Vatican secrecy, to assess, if only approximately, other aspects of Vatican finances, for instance those of Propaganda Fide or of Vatican investments in Italy. In this case, however, an assessment is practically impossible, both because of the irregular way the money comes in and because of the way it is administered. In a book I wrote in 1960 which contained something about Vatican finances, I assessed it tentatively and conservatively at $1\frac{1}{2}$ million, based on unofficial estimates gathered in Vatican quarters. Since then, the impact that Pope John's personality made on the world, the religious renewal provoked by the Ecumenical Council, the historical trips to Palestine, India, the United Nations and Fatima made by Paul VI have all helped to arouse among Catholics more interest for their church and contributions have risen accordingly. I am told that today an assessment of well over $4 or 5 million a year would be more in keeping with the situation.

Of all Vatican administrative bodies, the section of the State Secretariat that administers the fund is the one most closely and personally connected with the Pope. The fund, to use a military simile, is a kind of strategic reserve which the Pope or the Secretary of State use to meet sudden crises or to fill unexpected gaps. I shall quote just a few examples.

When Paul VI paid his visit to the sanctuary of Fatima, he made a speech to the Portuguese bishops and announced that the Holy See was contributing $150,000 to Portuguese foreign missions, $25,000 to the Patriarchate of Lisbon, $25,000 to the bishop of Leiria and $100,000—handed over to the nuncio—for the needs of the Church in Portugal in general. He disposed of $300,000 on this one occasion.

More recently the Vatican, at the peak of the Middle East crisis, gave large sums of money to help Arab refugees from Israel, the exact amount of which has not been disclosed, while previously $50,000 had been sent to help refugees both in North and South Vietnam. One can safely say that scarcely any calamity takes place in the world—wars, earthquakes, famines, epidemics, etc.—without the Catholic Church quickly concerning itself. In most cases the money is drawn at the shortest notice from the fund administered by the Secretariat of State.

Nearer home, I would mention that when in 1959 Pope John, following one of his sudden impulses, decided to raise the salaries of Vatican employees by about half and announced it as a *fait accompli*, a moment of embarrassment and uncertainty followed. Neither the governor of the Vatican City State, nor the Administration of the Holy See Patrimony, nor the Special Administration seemed capable, or rather willing, to produce the extra money. Finally the late Cardinal Domenico Tardini, then Secretary of State, who was also in favour of the rise, solved the problem by drawing on the special fund of the State Secretariat.

Likewise, most of the financial burden of the Ecumenical Council Vatican II, such as organization, travel expenses, living expenses for the most needy bishops during their stay in Rome, etc., was borne by the Secretariat of State. In this respect there was a pleasant surprise. The money budgeted to cover the first session of the Council turned out to be nearly enough to cover also the expenses of the second and third session.

As a last example I shall quote an episode that concerns the Vatican paper *Osservatore Romano*. When Pope Paul paid a visit to the slums of Rome, the editor of the paper, Raimondo Manzini, decided to print a special issue containing a colour supplement. Normally the expenses of the Vatican paper are borne by the Administration of the Holy See Patrimony, but the extra expense of a colour supplement had not been foreseen, so it looked as if Manzini's idea could not be carried out. Finally the State Secretariat intervened, almost at the last minute, with a cheque for ½ million lire.

In the Secretariat of State there is an unofficial 'aid commission' formed by a small group of prelates who examine and sift all the requests for financial help submitted to the Pope or the Secretary of State by welfare organizations, bishops, priests, religious orders and private individuals. In the most important cases the decision rests with the Secretary of State or with the Pope himself. Minor cases are handled by the committee. The interventions of the State Secretariat are not confined to emergencies and to dramatic cases. The fund is also used to help finance the building of churches, hospitals, schools, to support cultural institutions and to allow the Pope to dispense his private and often secret charity. Even in these cases the financial assistance provided by this fund goes beyond the normal routine and has an exceptional character.

Peter's Pence, in its contemporary form, represents the most direct and satisfactory relationship between the giver and the receiver. The faithful spontaneously donate to the successor of Peter according to their wealth, their generosity and their piety, and the Pope and his closest collaborators in the Secretariat of State redistribute the offerings as the needs for financial assistance arise, promptly and with the minimum of red tape. The actual bookkeeping of this considerable fund is carried out by two prelates and a layman typist.

Last year the Pope received about 30,000 requests for help from institutions or private people. Of these 6,000 special cases were handled directly by the aid commission mentioned above. The rest were taken care of by the following organizations: Caritas Internationalis, if the requests came from countries outside Italy; Pontifical Relief Organisation (Pontificia Opera di Assistenza, or POA) if they came from Italy; Apostolic Almonry if they concerned the city of Rome.

The Apostolic Almonry derives part of its funds from the Papal coffers and part from the souvenirs pilgrims and tourists buy in shops selling religious objects. The shopkeepers pay a fee to the Apostolic Almonry to have rosaries, crucifixes, photographs of the Pope, parchments with special prayers, Madonnas, etc., blessed by the Pope. The blessing, which is duly authenticated by a seal or label, increases the commercial value of the object and allows the shopkeepers to recoup the fee paid to the Almonry.

According to an official Vatican publication, the Pope's charity in the year 1966 involved several million dollars, but no precise figure was made available.

3

The Reverend Apostolic Chamber

The organization of the early societies of the faithful was simple. A paramount role was played by the apostles (the name in Greek meant 'messenger') or missionaries, sent out from the main centres of Christianity, like Jerusalem or Antioch, to spread the divine word. They travelled either alone or accompanied by assistants, to preach, establish new communities, comfort and reinforce in their faith already existing communities, give advice and eventually correct or condemn theological errors.

The local communities of Christians were called 'assemblies', following the pattern of the Jewish synagogues. The affairs of the communities were managed by a corps of elders (presbyters) who were either formally elected, or tacitly accepted by the community, or nominated by the travelling missionaries. The letters of Ignatius, bishop of Antioch, written in the first half of the second century, show that each church was ruled by one overseer (*episcopos* or bishop), assisted by a certain number of elders and assistants (*diakonos* or deacon).

The churches of the various cities were autonomous, keeping in touch by an exchange of letters and visits. In the very early days one of the current financial problems was to organize the communal evening meal, known as *agapè*, and in which the faithful partook of Christ's flesh (bread) and blood (wine). Later the meal was abolished and replaced by a more simple and symbolic function that took place in daytime. Justin explained about the Christians, in a letter to Emperor Antoninus Pius : 'Bread and wine mixed with water were brought to the bishop; he praised and honoured the Father of the Universe in the name of the Son and of the Holy Spirit and thanked God for having bestowed such gifts on us. The people reply by saying "amen". Then the deacons distribute to each of those present a portion of bread and wine and also take it to the members of the church who are not present.'[1] The letter sent by Justin to the emperor dispelled all sorts of strange and gruesome beliefs which the Pagans held about the Christians. The fact that they said they were drinking Christ's blood and eating his flesh, and the fact that at the end of the *agapè* they exchanged a 'kiss of peace', had led people to believe that the Christians were practising human sacrifice, cannibalism and indulging in sexual orgies.

Other expenses incurred by the early communities were the care of the poor and financing the trips of the missionaries to other cities and countries. There is not much known about the finances of the early communities, but some of the bishops must have been fairly wealthy if, in the frequent theological disputes that arose in those days, they were often accused of profiteering, greed and of leading luxurious lives. But probably both the wealth and the accusations were relative, as the whole standard of the early Christians was one of simplicity and austerity.

One must wait until Christianity was recognized as the official State religion by Emperor Constantine before one can speak of a centralized financial administration of the Catholic Church. From Constantine onwards the financial organization of the Church followed the pattern of the administrative machinery of the Roman Empire and was called *fiscus*. At the beginning of the eleventh century it took the name of 'Camera domini Papae' which later was changed into 'Camera Apostolica' (Apostolic chamber) and the person in charge of it took the name of Camerarius. The Apostolic chamber, to which still later the title of Reverend was added, continued to function as the administrative organ of the Church of Rome almost to the eve of the loss of temporal power. It therefore deserves to be described in some detail.

But before we do this, we should note that a fundamental change in Catholic finances took place when the Church became a temporal power or, to be more exact, added temporal power to the spiritual

---

[1] The word mass—*missa* in Latin—derives from this habit and is based on a misunderstanding. At the end of the function the bishop used to say: 'Ite, eucharistia missa est'. That is: 'Go, the eucharist has been sent'. This meant that the assistants or deacons were going to take the bread and wine to those who had been unable to attend. This was later shortened to 'Ite, missa est' and interpreted as meaning 'Go, the mass has come to an end'. *Missa*, which was originally a verb, thus became a noun.

power it already possessed. It was maintained during the Middle Ages, even by the Church herself, that the origin and the juridical foundation of temporal power was the so-called Donation of Constantine. It is a document dated 313 according to which Emperor Constantine, before leaving Rome for the East, donated to Pope Sylvester the city of Rome and the Italian provinces. The document describes in great detail the temporal possessions transferred under the jurisdiction of the Pope and attributes to the ecclesiastical hierarchy the same powers as a civil government. But it is a forgery, probably concocted in the days of Charlemagne, as historical mistakes contained in it have proved beyond doubt. Even the Catholic Church has recognized that the Donation of Constantine is a forgery and no longer considers it as a valid juridical title.

The bishop of Rome, after Constantine and until the reign of Pepin the Short (751–68), did exercise at intervals and in varying degrees some sort of temporal power over the city of Rome and the Italian provinces. But he was still the emperor's vassal and not a sovereign in his own right.

Ironically enough, while we have the complete text of the forged Donation of Constantine, we do not possess that of the real Donation that constituted the juridical basis of the Pope's temporal power. In 755–6 Pepin the Short, King of the Franks, conducted a campaign against the Lombards who had invaded the territories controlled by Rome. He was acting on a plea addressed to him in person by Pope Stephen II who, having realized that Rome could no longer rely on the protection of the decaying Byzantine Empire, had turned to the Frankish Kingdom in 753 to find a stronger protector. The tradition of French military and political interference in the affairs of the Catholic Church, either to protect or to threaten its possessions, which was to last for over one thousand years, was thus inaugurated.

Pepin the Short, when he had chased the Lombards out of the territories they had invaded and which the Pope was holding on behalf of Byzantium, donated the said territories to Stephen II. The sovereignty of the Pope is confirmed by the fact that from 781 onwards, under Pope Adrian I, the papal documents started bearing the date of the Pope's pontificate and not that of the Emperor of Byzantium nor of the King of France.

What was the role of the Apostolic Chamber in the administration? In the first place it administered the Papal Domains, which meant collecting taxes and customs from its subjects and bearing the expenses for defence, public order, public works, health, etc., just like any other State. It also controlled a quite considerable source of income from abroad. Since the ninth century, with the decadence of the Carolingian dynasty, many monasteries and churches with their annexed properties placed themselves under the protection of the Pope and paid to him, in exchange, an annual sum which was called *census*. The custom gradually spread to big landowners and finally to the new States that were born out of the dissolution of the Roman Empire.

In 1192 the Camerarius Cencio compiled the 'Liber censuum', that is the first complete list of all the sums the Holy See was entitled to receive from kings, princes, feudal lords, cities, castles, hostels, churches and monasteries. And as the funds increased, so did the importance and the size of the Apostolic Chamber that was administering them. To help the Camerlengo to carry out his job, a treasurer, a chief cashier and other officials were appointed. Around the middle of the fifteenth century the Vice-Camerlengo became also governor of the city of Rome, a charge he would retain for many centuries to come.

While the contributions from abroad fluctuated according to the political and military vicissitudes of the times, the papacy increased its temporal power. Roderigo Borgia, the brilliant and ruthless Spaniard who sat on the throne of Peter from 1492 to 1503 with the name of Alexander VI, played a large part in this. The vast estates of the great Roman families, the Colonna, Gaetani and Savelli, were expropriated and their fortunes seized. The Pope also inherited, according to the law, from several cardinals some of whom, like Cardinal Michiel and Cardinal Orsini, were almost certainly murdered at the Pope's instigation.

But it was Cesare Borgia, the bastard son the Pope had had from Vannozza Cattanei, who greatly extended the territorial possession of the Holy See. This young, handsome, ruthless, cunning and intrepid military leader and statesman, conquered by bravery, diplomatic ability and by treachery the Romagna and the duchies of Urbino and Camerino. As a matter of fact, Cesare's conquests and the expropriations of the fiefs of the big Roman families by his father were nominally carried out on behalf of the Church but were in effect intended as personal acquisitions to the house of Borgia.

But when, after the death of Alexander VI and after the short interlude of Pius III, the lifelong enemy of the Borgia, Giuliano della Rovere, became Pope, he quickly exiled Cesare Borgia and annexed all his possessions to the Holy See. Julius II, the Pope who had himself portrayed in a cuirass and helmet, personally followed the campaigns of his army and, besides reconquering the territories that belonged to Cesare Borgia, he enlarged the conquest even farther and established the boundaries of the Papal States as they were, more or less, to remain, despite all sorts of vicissitudes, until 1870.

Julius II also established the tradition of the Roman Pontiff as a patron of the arts. During the ten years of his reign (1503–13) Rome experienced a spectacular flowering of architecture, painting, sculpture and literature. He laid the foundation stone of St Peter's on a project drawn by Bramante. The same Bramante built the Vatican Palace. On the Pope's commission Michelangelo painted the ceiling of the Sistine Chapel and sculpted the Moses, while Raphael painted the frescoes of the Stanze. All this, evidently, cost a great deal of money.

His successor, Leo X, continued to play the role of Maecenas in an almost obsessive way. There was scarcely a poet, writer, philosopher or painter, however mediocre, who did not receive papal encouragement and often a well-paid job in his court. He used to spend an average of 100,000 ducats a year, almost double that of his predecessor.

Leo X had 683 courtiers and servants, ranging from the archbishop-almoner to the keepers of elephants, from the court composer to the buffoons with whom he himself liked to jest. He loved hunting and used to leave Rome, sometimes for several weeks, followed by two hundred riders, among whom there were cardinals, musicians and comedians. He was also a great music-lover, composed music himself and kept a permanent orchestra. He bought precious instruments and published the score of a collection of the fifteen most beautiful masses of those days, the 'Liber quindecim missarum'. He kept a permanent theatrical company which performed, among hundreds of other plays, the rather pornographic and irreverent *La Mandragola* by Machiavelli.

The Church of Rome was to pay rather heavily, in the religious field, for this lavish spending. The need for more and more money induced Julius II and Leo X to push the sale of benefices and indulgences to such extremes that it provoked Luther's revolt and the Reformation. It is a tragic paradox to think that the building of St Peter's, the biggest church in the world and the symbol of Catholic power, and the magnificent flourishing of the arts in Rome, should have caused such a serious and still unhealed rift in European Christianity.

The occasion of the rift was accidental and the consequences went far beyond the intentions of the characters involved. Julius II who, as we saw, had embarked on the gigantic task of building St Peter's, had published in 1510 a bull offering special indulgences, *in forma jubilaei,* to those who would contribute financially to the enterprise. His successor Leo X entrusted the archbishop of Mainz with the task of issuing the indulgences and collecting the relative funds in the provinces of Mainz, Magdeburg and in the diocese of Halberstadt. Curiously enough, the Pope thought it would have been unwise to spread the initiative to Spain, France or England. One can only wonder what would have happened to Catholicism if the sale of indulgences had been extended to Spain and France (England was about to break loose anyhow for other reasons) with the same counter-effect it had in Germany.

The archbishop of Mainz entrusted the sale of indulgences to a Dominican by the name of Tetzel who was renowned for his oratory. According to the instructions imparted to Father Tetzel by the archbishop, and which he in turn had received from Rome, there were four different types of indulgence, each of which could be bought separately. The two main ones were :

1 A plenary indulgence for all sins committed, including their expiation in Purgatory, which could be acquired by visiting, after confession and repentance, at least seven churches bearing the papal coat-of-arms, and reciting in each of them five paternosters and five Ave Marias and paying, *dulcis in fundo,* a sum varying from one to twenty-five gold florins.

2 A plenary remission of all the sins committed by a deceased person whose soul was in Purgatory, which could be acquired after a donation was made in proportion to the wealth of the person interceding in favour of the deceased.

A young theology professor of the University of Wittenberg, Martin Luther, was outraged by this practice and affixed on the doors of the castle which house the university the famous ninety-five theses. It was merely an invitation to start an academic discussion, but it ended by sparking off the Reformation.

But where did the Vatican find the vast amount of money needed to cover the ambitious building programmes, the sumptuous way of life indulged in by the Renaissance Popes or the military expenses of the crusades? The taxes collected from the citizens of the Papal Domains, Peter's Pence, customs, excises, the sale of indulgences and other more or less normal sources of revenue, were not enough. Therefore the Popes embarked on a peculiar, adventurous and, to our modern minds, absolutely preposterous financial operation. They started selling offices—that is, the jobs in the Reverend Apostolic Chamber, in the papal court, in the army, in the administration of the Papal Domains, in the police, in the administration of justice, etc.—for ready cash.

Those who were interested in the deal put down in cash the amount required, bought the job and were assured of receiving a regular salary, or annuity, for the rest of their lives. The Apostolic Chamber paid the salaries out of the taxes exacted, the tributes received from abroad and other revenues. But soon it was found that the revenues were not sufficient to pay the annuities, and therefore more offices were sold. It became a vicious circle.

According to Leopold von Ranke, in the year 1471, under the pontificate of Sixtus IV, the Holy See had 650 offices to sell, out of which it could get approximately 100,000 scudi. Sixtus IV gradually sold them all and when he again became short of cash he created and sold more offices. Secretaries, notaries, procurators, scribes, recorders, archivists, copyists, messengers and ushers started mushrooming almost overnight. His successor, Innocent VIII, who was once so short of money that he had to pawn the Papal tiara, founded a college of secretaries for which he was paid 60,000 scudi, plus many more other offices.

His successor, Alexander VI, nominated eighty writers of briefs who paid 750 scudi each. Julius II did the same for one hundred clerks of the archives, who also paid 750 scudi each. But it was Leo X, always short of money because of his extravagant way of life, who pushed the sale of offices to extremes. He appointed numbers of Cardinals, from whom he extorted a great deal of money, but he also created and sold no less than 1,200 new offices. These officials often had curious names, like Knights of St Peter, *portionarii*, squires, Jannissaries, but no duties to perform. This meant that by buying the office, they not only received a good annuity but also some minor privileges or titles of distinction. By this method Leo X collected about 900,000 scudi. All told, under his reign, the number of offices reached the figure of 2,150 and the total annuities to be paid to their holders mounted to 320,000 scudi a year.

The holders of more important offices, like that of Camerlengo, or Governor of the City of Rome, of high administrative official in the Apostolic Chamber, of treasurer, fiscal judge, etc., who had had to pay very heavily for their position, were naturally inclined to try and recover the capital they had advanced in all sorts of dubious ways. This encouraged craft and corruption.

There were, however, redeeming features: the golden prospects of investing in a Vatican office attracted to Rome many wealthy people who spent a great deal of money, gave work to servants and artisans and brought new life to the otherwise stagnant economy of the Eternal City. The system also permitted Leo X to be lenient in taxing the citizens of the Papal Domains, and this leniency helped their economic development. The heavy taxation, gradually increased to the point of becoming unbearable and of causing uprisings, was to come later.

Of Leo X it has been said that he wasted the revenues of three pontificates: that of his predecessor, his own and that of his successor to whom he left nothing but debts. Leo X also borrowed large sums of money in a private capacity: 32,000 scudi from Alvise Gaddi, 200,000 from Bernardo Bini, more money from various friends like Salviati or Ridolfi and even from his own servants. They were never paid back and some of them were utterly ruined.

Adrian VI, who succeeded Leo X in 1522, and who was the last non-Italian Pope, tried to restore some kind of order in Vatican finances and embarked on a policy of strict economy. Adrian Florenz was born in Utrecht in 1459 from poor parents, was an extremely learned and austere man and had been the tutor of Charles V who supported his election. He abolished the sale of offices, drastically reduced the pomp and splendour of the court and sacked hundreds of parasites. The Romans hated him both for being a foreigner and for being parsimonious. The Curia felt the same and used to the full its delaying tactics in order to obstruct his reforms. Ironically enough, when he started preparing an expedition against the Turks who were threatening Hungary, he once again had to resort to the sale of offices. He died after a reign of one year and seven months, an embittered and disillusioned man. On his tomb, in the German church of Santa Maria dell'Anima (St Mary of the Soul), there is the following sad epitaph he himself dictated: 'Alas! how important, even for the best of men, is the epoch in which his activity takes place'.

The next Pope was Giulio dei Medici, nephew of Lorenzo the Magnificent, who took the name of Clement VII (1523–34). This pontificate witnessed many disasters for the Catholic Church: the sack of Rome by the mercenaries of the Constable of Bourbon (1527); the capture of the Pope who was released only after having paid a heavy ransom; the spreading of the Protestant revolt in Germany and the establishment of the Anglican Church; and the conversion of Scandinavia and part of Switzerland to Protestantism. A third of Christianity ceased to be Catholic. Despite these tragic events, the papal tradition of lavish spending on the arts continued and Michelangelo sculpted the tomb of the Medici in Florence and painted the Universal Judgment in Rome.

To return to Vatican finances during the Renaissance: while the sale of offices continued, it was flanked by another peculiar form of money-raising, the sale of the *monti*. The word *monte* meant a regular source of income, like for instance the impost on flour, on salt, on olive oil, or the tax on buildings, or the revenue of customs, etc. The Apostolic Chamber, having assessed what each of these *monti* was likely to bring in, sold them to contractors, entirely or in part, for a lump sum. Some of the *monti* were *vacabili*, which meant that after a certain number of years, usually nine, or at the death of the contractor, the revenues reverted to the Apostolic Chamber. Others were *non vacabili*, which meant that the right to collect the revenue, at the death of the contractor, went to his heirs.

In order to be able to sell the *monti*, the Apostolic Chamber, with the Pope's approval, created more sources of revenue, that is, in effect, more taxes, or imposts, or customs on goods that were previously exempted. The total revenue of the Apostolic Chamber increased at the rate shown below. Not all the Popes of this period are included because for some of their pontificates there are no reliable details available.

Revenues of the Apostolic Chamber

Julius II (1503–13)	350,000	scudi a year
Leo X (1513–21)	420,000	,, ,, ,,
Clement VII (1523–34)	500,000	,, ,, ,,
Paul III (1534–49)	706,473	,, ,, ,,
Paul IV (1555–59)	700,000	,, ,, ,,
Pius V (1566–72)	898,482	,, ,, ,,
Gregory XIII (1572–85)	1,100,000	,, ,, ,,

The figures quoted above are in most cases approximate and they refer to only one year in the pontificates of each of the Popes mentioned, but still they reveal the general trend very clearly. But although the revenues of the Apostolic Chamber were more than trebled in the seventy-two years, papal finances were no healthier than before. The reason, of course, was that a large part of the revenue went to pay the annuities and part of the remainder never reached the coffers of the Apostolic Chamber because it had already been sold to the contractors of the *monti*. Thus, for instance, the customs of the city of Rome alone yielded the considerable sum of 133,000 scudi in the year 1576. Of this, however, 111,170 scudi were pocketed by the contractors and the Apostolic Chamber, after some further deductions, received only 13,000 scudi, that is 10 per cent. The system of selling the *monti* was extended to all the Papal States, so that many provinces were no longer sending any money to Rome.

Gregory XIII (1572–85) was a spender like his predecessors, but he did not want to increase the already very heavy taxation. Therefore, being a jurist, he resorted to a legal method to raise money. The archives of the Vatican were carefully explored and the feudal titles of tenure punctiliously examined. If they were found to be faulty, either because a fief had been granted to a family whose direct line had become extinct, or because the vassal had stopped paying tribute to the Holy See, or for some other pretext, the estates concerned were seized, often by force.

Gregory XIII proudly claimed that by this method he had increased the revenue of the Holy See by 100,000 scudi a year. The method, however, had its disadvantages. Many of the big families, especially in the provinces, refused to be peremptorily dispossessed of the estates they had held for centuries and often took to arms. A state of anarchy resulted, banditry became widespread and only the iron hand of Sixtus V succeeded in restoring order.

Of Sixtus V (1585–90) it has been said that he reigned five years, built five bridges and five churches, erected five obelisks and left five million gold scudi to the Church. The latter is what interests us most, especially as it was a rather unusual financial operation.

Ranke discovered in the archives of the Chigi family in Rome a kind of diary or log-book kept by Sixtus V when he was a poor Franciscan preacher and which contains some interesting details about his first humble financial deals. We find that his brother-in-law Battista bought on his behalf twelve sheep, for which the future Pope paid in instalments until they became his. The sheep were kept by the brother-in-law and the two divided the profit equally. The log-book shows how he saved little sums of money and administered them carefully, gradually increasing his capital to 200 florins. It was with the same precision and administrative skill that Sixtus V ran the finances of the Holy See.

The capital he left at his death amounted to not quite five million scudi. A year after his election he had already collected one million scudi in gold, in 1587 a second million and in 1588 a third. Each time he made a million he placed it in the coffers of Castel Sant'Angelo, the powerful fortress linked to the Vatican by a fortified passage, and, in the course of a solemn ceremony, dedicated it to the Virgin Mary and to the Apostles Peter and Paul. Part of the papal bull concerning this treasure reads:

> The Pope considers not only the waves which sometimes rock the barque of Peter, but also the storms that threaten from a distance: the hatred of the heretics is implacable; the powerful Turk, Assuerus, the scourge of divine wrath, threatens the faithful; and God to whom the Pope entrusts himself in these perils has admonished him that the father of the family must

keep a vigil also at night. He follows the example of the fathers of the Old Testament who used to keep a considerable sum of money in the temple of the Lord.

Sixtus V laid down very strictly the emergencies in which his successors were allowed to draw on the treasure : a crusade to conquer the Holy Land; a general war of all Christian nations against the Turks; a famine or plague; the danger of losing a Catholic province; an attack against the Papal States, or when there was a chance of the Holy See itself conquering a city. He threatened his successors with the wrath of God and of the Apostles Peter and Paul should they use the treasure for other purposes.[2]

This remarkable man had been elected as a transition and compromise Pope, because it was thought that he was in poor health. But, immediately after the election, he threw away the walking stick on which he had been leaning so heavily during the Conclave and called in the executioner. He exterminated banditry with a ruthlessness which has remained proverbial and decreed the death penalty for incest, abortion, sodomy and adultery.

He completely reorganized the Roman Curia on the lines which, despite several subsequent reforms, are fundamentally extant today. He created a papal navy to defend the coasts against the raids of the pirates. His energy and his drive were responsible for many ambitious building projects. It was he, for instance, who ordered that the building of St Peter's dome be resumed on the original plan by Michelangelo, twenty-five years after the death of the master. The town planning of the historical centre of Rome owes much to him.

Because of all these remarkable achievements, also by the accumulation of nearly five million scudi in the coffers of Castel Sant'Angelo, his reign has been favourably looked upon by posterity. But if one delves a little deeper into the financial juggling by which the treasure was assembled, one may express some doubts. Sixtus V did carry out considerable economies and increased the revenues. But, according to his own statements, the diminished expenses of the Apostolic Chamber amounted to only 146,000 scudi a year and the

---

[2] The events mentioned above took place only too frequently and the treasure assembled by Sixtus V was gradually spent by later Popes and never replaced.

net revenue of the Holy See increased by only 350,000 scudi a year. Just enough to cover his building programmes, but certainly not enough to accumulate the vast treasure of Castel Sant'Angelo.

How, then, did he do it? Simply by extending the old system of creating new offices and selling them, increasing taxation, creating new *monti* on the new taxes and selling them too.

He certainly showed great financial skill in his operations. Take for instance the important office of Treasurer of the Apostolic Chamber. Before Sixtus it went for 15,000 gold scudi. He sold it to a member of the Giustiniani family for 50,000, then nominated Giustiniani a Cardinal and sold it again to a Pepoli for 72,000. Shortly afterwards he gave a red hat also to Pepoli and then assigned half of the income of this office, namely 5,000 scudi a year, to a new *monte*, which he sold for 50,000 scudi. All told, he pocketed 172,000 scudi against a promise to pay 5,000 a year, that is at a reasonable rate of interest of about 2.9 per cent.

But it isn't as simple as that. In practice the deal included the appointment of two new Cardinals with all the apanages involved which reduces the profit made by the Holy See quite considerably. And it still meant borrowing money at an interest.

Looked at in a more general perspective, Sixtus V started selling many offices which before were freely given, including very important ones such as that of commissary, solicitor to the Apostolic Chamber, advocate of the poor, etc. He invented many more offices, such as those of twenty-four referendaries and of notaries in the main cities of the Papal Domains. He also formed new *monti* : three *non vacabili* and eight *vacabili*, which was more than any of his predecessors had done.

The *monti* were based on new taxes, including some that hit the most hard-working and poorest classes of the people (for example those who used horses and buffaloes to drag barges up-stream), on essential commodities like firewood and wine sold in retail. Strangely enough, he was advised in these operations by a Portuguese Jew by the name of Lopez who had fled from Portugal for fear of the Inquisition.

That the Church needed a fund or reserve to meet emergencies goes without doubt. But, as Ranke neatly put it : 'To borrow money and impose heavy imposts, merely for the purpose of locking up the proceeds in a fortress, as a treasure for some future contingency, this is altogether foreign to the general practice of governments.' I would only venture to comment that Sixtus himself, being a shrewd administrator, perhaps realised the unsoundness of the operation but also thought that, judging by how things had been going, such a reserve was a necessity. One can also say that, if he did considerably increase what we would today call the national debt, he did not do it in order to squander money on elephants, theatrical companies or buffoons. He too, however, was not immune from nepotism, a plague that afflicted the papacy until modern times.

The frequent wars, either defensive or aimed at enlarging the Papal States, the crusades, the expeditions against the Turks in the Balkans, the defence of the coasts of Italy against pirates and the grandiose building projects and encouragement given to the arts, no doubt absorbed a great part of the Holy See revenues. With a certain amount of goodwill these expenses, and even the debts incurred, could be understood and justified.

But what is hard to tolerate is nepotism. Even Sixtus V, the parsimonious Franciscan, nominated one of his great-nephews Cardinal and assigned to him ecclesiastic revenues amounting to 100,000 scudi. To another he conferred the titles and the estates of Marquis of Mentana, Prince of Venafro and Count of Celano.

Clement VIII (Aldobrandini) donated to his nephews during thirteen years of reign over one million scudi in cash. Paul V (Borghese) gave his nephews 689,727 scudi in cash, 24,600 scudi in *monti* (nominal value) and 268,176 scudi in offices, the last figure being reckoned on what they would have had to pay if they had bought them instead of getting them for nothing. He also gave them high, extremely well-paid jobs in the administration as well as the principality of Sulmona, palaces and villas in Rome and its neighbourhood, plus all kinds of privileges and exemption from taxes. The Borghese family became in this way the richest in Rome.

The same story, in varying degrees, applies to many other princely families whose enormous fortunes were founded by their relationship to a Pope and favours received from him. The Colonna, Orsini, Ludovisi, della Rovere, Farnese, Barberini, Boncompagni, Pamphilj, Odescalchi, Pignatelli, Albani are the most outstanding examples.

The practice of nepotism reached such a degree that Urban VIII (1623–44), a Barberini, felt some qualms (or perhaps he wanted to appease public opinion?) and appointed, in 1640, a special committee to investigate whether what he had done to favour his family was legitimate or not. The committee, unsurprisingly, established the principle that the capacity of pontiff and that of sovereign were joined in the same person and that the Pope, as a temporal ruler, was entitled to donate to his family the savings he made or the surplus of the State revenues. The fact that the revenues were not nearly sufficient and that the Holy See was getting more and more in debt was overlooked. The opinion expressed by the committee was endorsed by the General of the Jesuits, Father Vitelleschi.

The reconciliation of Christ and Mammon had thus received the official rubber-stamp. Divine providence was a good thing, but human providence was not bad either.

Maffeo Barberini, alias Urban VIII, made his brother Antonio and his three nephews, Francesco, Antonio and Lorenzo Magalotti, Cardinals (the latter was a son of his sister). The three sons of his brother Antonio, that is Francesco, Antonio and Taddeo, became respectively Camerlengo, vice-chancellor and prefect in the papal government. They held the key posts of the Establishment and had an assured income, all told, of at least half a million scudi a year. This without counting the ecclesiastical benefices, the estates, the gifts in ready cash bestowed on them by their uncle.

But nepotism, naturally enough, was not only confined to the Popes but spread down the whole hierarchy. Cardinals, bishops, abbots, generals of religious orders, high executives in the Apostolic Chamber, down to the humble parish priests, did everything in their power to enrich or place in good jobs their brothers, nephews or other relatives. The total damage caused by nepotism to the Church of Rome is impossible to assess.

One might even assume that, had it not been for nepotism, for the building mania that possessed so many Popes, for the splendour of the Roman court and for a certain happy-go-lucky inclination to borrow today and forget the debt tomorrow, the Church of Rome could easily have avoided the financial troubles in which it was almost chronically involved. That it could have avoided being so hopelessly in debt and being compelled to tax its subjects in such a ferocious way as to give rise to the opinion that to be a subject of the Pope was a misfortune rather than a privilege. But history is not made of 'ifs'.

What happened is that the debt continued to rise steadily as shown in the table below, which also compares the revenues and the interest paid on the debts. All the figures are in scudi.

	Debt	Revenue	Interest
1587	6,500,000	1,358,456	715,913
1592	12,242,620	1,585,520	1,088,600
1623	18,000,000	1,818,104	1,800,000?
1635	30,000,000	....	3,000,000?
1644	38,000,000	2,200,000	3,800,000?
1655	48,000,000	....	4,800,000?
1670	52,000,000	....	5,200,000?

The question marks placed next to the figures in the interest column indicate that there are no sure details available. They have been tentatively put down on the knowledge that the Apostolic Chamber paid on average an interest of about 10 per cent on the money it borrowed.

While in 1587 about half the revenue went to pay the interest, in 1592 three-quarters of the revenue was absorbed by the interest and in 1623, when the interest must have risen to about 1,800,000, the whole revenue disappeared. In 1644, when the revenue had risen to 2,200,000 scudi and the interest could be assessed at around 3,800,000, the revenue was not sufficient to pay the interest. From then on the interest was paid by getting more into debt.

A quite logical and sound attempt to stop this hopeless situation was made by Alexander VII (1655–67) at the beginning of his pontificate. Instead of selling more offices or *monti*, he borrowed money directly from bankers at an interest of 4 per cent and redeemed all the *monti vacabili* on which the Apostolic Chamber was paying an interest of 10.5 per cent. Because of the very high rate of interest, the market value of the *monti* was much higher than the nominal value. A *monte* which had been bought for 100 scudi was valued at about 150 scudi. Alexander VII redeemed them at their market value, but he still made a good deal because he had to pay an interest of 6 per cent instead of 10 per cent.[3]

[3] A similar operation was repeated at the present time by Cardinal Spellman with the mortgages of the diocese of New York.

Alexander VII then decided to redeem the *monti non vacabili* which yielded more than 4 per cent. These he did not redeem at their market value but at their nominal value. To repeat the example made above, a *monte non vacabile* bought for 100 was valued at about 116. Again a sound business deal. But it was only a short interlude after which Vatican finances again fell into the costly habit of selling offices and *monti*.

A move similar to that of Alexander VII was made in 1692 by Innocent XII (1691–1700) who in his constitution *Ad hoc unxit* abolished the sale of the offices of the Reverend Apostolic Chamber, and more precisely those of General Auditor, General Treasurer, of the twelve clerics and of their President. He also ordered that they should be refunded the 1,020,716 scudi they had paid for the offices. This figure gives a clear indication of how important these offices must have been. In this case the reform introduced by Innocent XII was not so much of a financial but of a technical and, one might say, moral character. He did not want to entrust the difficult and delicate task of administrating the Apostolic Chamber (which was similar to a Council of Ministers in a modern State) to men who had achieved the position merely by money and not talent or ability.

Further technical reforms were introduced in the organization of the Apostolic Chamber first in 1735 by Clement XII who had been himself General Treasurer before being elected Pope, and in 1746 by his successor, Benedict XIV. The two reforms brought about a much more precise, detailed and periodical method of accounting. The General Treasurer, apart from having to give a detailed account at fixed dates of all sums received and spent, was also entrusted with the task of investigating cases of smuggling, of frauds, of wills made in favour of the Church and not executed by the heirs, of controlling the tax collectors and giving judgment in these matters. The General Treasurer was also appointed General Collector of taxes, Superintendent of customs, head of St Angel's Castle and General Commissary for the sea.

The Pope used to choose personally among the clerics of the Reverend Apostolic Chamber, who had no longer bought the office, the heads of the Annona (food supplies in general), of the Grascia (meat, fats, olive oil, fish and fixing the prices of such commodities), of the roads, of the archives and of the river banks. The other posts, such as head of the jails, of the mint, of the customs, of the army and of the sea (the fleet, lighthouses, observation towers and fortresses were under the control of the General Commissary for the sea) were drawn by lots annually among the other clerics of the Apostolic Chamber.

It would be too long and repetitious to follow all the vicissitudes of Vatican finances until modern times. But I would like to give the reader an account, even if only a sketchy one, of a few main events which had a bearing on financial affairs and which preceded that most decisive event : the loss of temporal power in 1870.

Temporal power had in effect already been lost in January 1798 when General Berthier, acting on Bonaparte's orders, occupied Rome, proclaimed the republic and declared Pius VI deposed as a temporal sovereign. A year before the Pope had been compelled to sign the treaty of Tolentino in which he had renounced the papal domain of Avignon and pledged to pay to France 46 million scudi. Pius VI died in August 1799 as he was being dragged to France as a prisoner.

The Papal States were restored by Napoleon to his successor Pius VII by the treaty of Lunéville in 1801 and again taken away in 1809 when the French troops reconquered Rome, arrested the Pope and exiled him to Savona. In 1814, before facing for the last time the coalition of his enemies, Napoleon sent Pius VII back to Rome and reinstated him in his territorial possessions.

Despite all these dramatic events, the finances of the Vatican, in 1814, were in a fairly sound state. The revenue was 1,852,760 scudi and the expenses 1,345,136 scudi. In reality the revenue must be reduced by about 30 per cent, which was the cost of collection, but still revenues and expenses balanced each other. From then on, however, both the revenues, that is in practice the taxes imposed on the Pope's subjects, and the expenses started running away, with expenses definitely in the lead. All the figures are in scudi.[4]

---

[4] Between 1814–34 the scudo weighed 26.428 grams of silver; between 1835–66 it weighed 26.698 grams of silver.

	Revenues	*Expenses*
1814	1,852,760	1,546,136
1820	6,730,271	7,004,844
1830	8,547,452	8,775,120
1840	9,263,369	9,798,946
1846	9,800,093	10,679,331

Here again one must remember to reduce the revenues by 30 per cent, so that in 1846, for instance, the deficit amounted to about 3 million scudi. This being the situation, it was inevitable for the Holy See to continue making recourse to credit or other exceptional means. The mounting expenses were partly met, in the period examined, by the sale of property belonging to the Apostolic Chamber, by the sale of the property of the House of Leuchtenberg which the Holy See had inherited and by asking the various contractors who were running the customs, the collection of taxes, the salt and tobacco monopolies etc., on behalf of the Apostolic Chamber, to pay a deposit as a guarantee. It was somewhat similar to the old sale of offices, with the difference that, in the case of the deposits, the Vatican was not required to pay interest.

But the main new feature of Vatican borrowing was the recourse to the big financial houses outside the Papal States, and especially the Rothschilds of Paris. Here are the most important loans (all the figures are in scudi), contracted by the Holy See between 1831 and 1846:

Date and name of lender	Nominal value	Price of issue	Commission	Sum received
15 December 1831 with Rothschild of Paris	3,000,000	65%	3%	1,860,000
10 August 1832 with Rothschild of Paris	3,000,000	72½%	2%	2,115,000
15 September 1833 with Rothschild of Paris	3,000,000	82%	2%	2,400,000
15 March 1837 with Rothschild of Paris	1,000,000	95%	3%	925,000
3 August 1837 with Rothschild of Paris	2,000,000	95%	3%	1,850,000
20 January 1846 with Torlonia of Rome and Parodi of Genoa	2,000,000	95%	2%	1,860,000
Total scudi	14,000,000			11,110,000

On these loans the Holy See had to pay an interest of 5 per cent a year on the nominal value plus 1 per cent for amortization. But if one considers the gap between the nominal value and the price of issue, plus the commission, especially of the usurious first deal concluded with the Rothschilds, the interest became much higher.

The economic and political situation in the Papal States went from bad to worse. Taxation reached unbearable limits, agriculture, industry and commerce stagnated while revolts flared up in many provinces and were ruthlessly suppressed with the help of Austrian troops. In the Romagna a tribunal presided over by Cardinal Agostino Rivarola sentenced to death, to jail for life or to perpetual exile 508 people in one court sitting. They included thirty aristocrats, 156 landowners and merchants, two priests, seventy-four office workers, thirty-eight soldiers, sixty-two doctors, lawyers, architects and intellectuals and 146 artisans, which shows that all classes were united in their opposition to the papal rule. There was no freedom of the press nor of speech, books were censored and usually banned, universities were closed down. Leo XII (1823–29) forbade vaccination against smallpox as being against nature. The Jews were again locked inside the ghettos.

The muddle in the central administration reached spectacular proportions. Between 1835 and 1845, while Monsignor Tosti was General Treasurer of the Apostolic Chamber, no budget was drawn up. His successor, Monsignor Antonelli (later a Cardinal and Secretary of State), instructed the chief accountant Angelo Galli to reconstruct the budgets of the ten preceding years. It took him two and a half years.

The Papal States were so badly, so despotically and narrow-mindedly run and its subjects had reached such a state of exasperation that the big powers of Europe became alarmed by the danger of an explosion of popular wrath. They met in conference and prepared a Memorandum which was delivered on 10 May 1831 and in which the Holy See was formally invited to mend its ways. The Memorandum suggested, among other things, the institution of municipal and provincial councils elected by the people, an improvement in the judicial system, the admission of laymen to the administration of the State and of Justice and the setting up of a 'Court of Accounts', that is a body to control the financial operations of the various Vatican offices. What a come-down from the days of Innocent III when the Pope ruled over Emperors, Kings, Princes and feudal lords!

Gregory XVI (1831–46) accepted the Memorandum in principle and started carrying out some of the reforms suggested. But he did it in a very half-hearted way. For instance, he instituted the municipal councils but, instead of allowing the people to elect the councillors, they were appointed by the government. Everybody was dissatisfied and when the Austrian troops left, the revolt flared up again. Again the Austrians were called in and severe repressions carried out by the papal police and the Memorandum was completely forgotten.

His successor, Pius IX (1846–78), began his pontificate by granting an amnesty for all political crimes. He was acclaimed as a liberal and a patriot and many people envisaged a unified Italy, freed from the foreign yoke and placed under the rule and the protection of the Pope. True to this image, he proclaimed a constitution, formed a Senate of Rome and entrusted all State affairs to a Council of Ministers, all laymen. The Reverend Apostolic Chamber, which had been the pivot of the entire Holy See administrative machinery for eight centuries, ceased to have any importance. It has, however, survived to our day and carries out the routine administration of the Holy See during the *Sede vacante*, that is from the death of a Pope to the election of a new one.

The reforms introduced by Pius IX were too late to have any effect. The Pope, who at the beginning of his reign had been hailed as a prospective saviour of Italy, was now siding with Austria and opposing the war of independence. Riots broke out also in Rome and in 1848 the Pope fled to Gaeta, on the border of the kingdom of Naples. The Romans proclaimed a republic. In April 1850 Pius IX returned to Rome under the protection of French bayonets. But the end was getting near.

In December 1869 Pius IX solemnly inaugurated an Ecumenical Council (known as Vatican Council I) which was to proclaim the dogma of the Pope's infallibility. In this respect, and referring to the sorry state of Vatican finances, he remarked wittily : 'Sarò forse infallibile, ma sono certamente fallito'. ('I may be infallible, but I am certainly bankrupt'—*fallito* in Italian.)

When Napoleon III was defeated by the Prussians at Sedan, the Pope lost his chief defender and the King of Italy, Victor Emmanuel II, took advantage of the situation and invaded the Papal States. Pius IX appealed to Austria and Prussia, but without result. The defence of Rome was short-lived. On 20 September 1870 the guns of General Cadorna opened a breach in the Aurelian Wall near the Porta Pia and the plumed Bersaglieri streamed through it and occupied the Eternal City. The temporal power of the Church of Rome had come to an end for good.

4

Mussolini's Concordat

Seen in retrospect, the loss of temporal power was one of the best things that could have happened to the Church of Rome.

In the first place it put an end to a government that was inefficient, despotic, narrow-minded, hated by its own subjects and, as the Memorandum of the big powers showed, despised even abroad. An inert, cumbersome, out-dated institution which, because of its own weakness and because of the powerful and active social, political, nationalistic, ideological and economic forces that were reshaping Europe, was doomed anyhow. King Victor Emmanuel II of Italy, by conquering the Papal States, spared the Pope the indignity of being expelled by his own subjects or, at best, the embarrassment of retaining a precarious throne by virtue of foreign troops.

In the second place the papacy, having lost temporal power, gained a greater impartiality, and being no longer mixed up in international and internal politics, was, to a great extent, relieved of financial worries and entanglements and therefore able to exercise more effectively its spiritual power. What the Church of Rome lost in the material sphere, she gained in the moral and spiritual one.

But Pius IX did not quite see it that way. He locked himself up inside the Vatican in self-imposed and disdainful imprisonment, excommunicated King Victor Emmanuel and all those who had contributed to the occupation of the Papal States and forbade all Catholics to collaborate with the 'usurper' or to take part, either as candidates or as voters, in any kind of election. To all attempts by the Italian Government to reach a reconciliation, or at least a *modus vivendi*, he replied with the famous 'Non possumus'.

In 1871 the Italian Parliament approved the so-called 'Law of Guarantees', intended as an act of good will and a sign of friendship. Article One said, 'The person of the Supreme Pontiff is sacred and inviolable.' It went on to offer various guarantees and privileges to the Holy See, including complete freedom in the exercise of its spiritual power, diplomatic immunity to Vatican diplomats and to diplomats of foreign countries accredited to the Holy See, the right to keep a small private army in the Vatican and, curiously enough, the privilege granted to the Pope to use the Italian postal and telegraph service free of charge.

On the financial side, the Law of Guarantees, Article Four, stated : 'The annual income of 3,225,000 lire will continue to be allotted in favour of the Holy See.' This referred to the sum which, in the last budget of the papal administration, before the occupation of Rome, was assigned to the immediate needs of the Pope himself, his entourage and household, and the Roman Curia. It is interesting to note that in 1866 the Holy See had carried out a monetary reform transforming the scudi into lire of the same value of Italian lire at the rate of 1 scudo to 5.375 lire. The new silver coin weighed 5 grams.

As the Law of Guarantees explained :

> This sum, which is the equivalent of that inscribed in the budget under the headings : Sacred Apostolic palaces, Sacred College of Cardinals, Ecclesiastical Congregations, Secretariat of State and Diplomatic Corps abroad, will be granted in order to meet the needs of the Supreme Pontiff and the various ecclesiastical needs of the Holy See, for the ordinary and extraordinary upkeep and custody of the Apostolic palaces and their annexes; for the gratuities and pensions granted to the guards mentioned above and to the members of the Pontifical Court and to sundry expenses; plus the ordinary and extraordinary upkeep of the Museums and Library and to the salaries and pensions of their employees.
>
> The above-mentioned sum will be inscribed in the Grand Book of Public Debt, in a perpetual and inalienable form, in the name of the Holy See; and during the vacancy of the Holy See it will continue to be paid to meet the needs of the Roman Church in the interval.
>
> It will be exempt from all kinds of taxes and dues of a governmental, communal or provincial character; and it will never be reduced, even if the Italian government should subsequently decide to take over the expenses concerning the Museums and the Library.

Article Five further specified that:

> The Supreme Pontiff, apart from the revenue mentioned in the preceding article, will continue to enjoy the Vatican and Lateran palaces, with all their buildings, gardens and ground annexed, and the villa of Castelgandolfo with all its annexes.
>
> The above mentioned palaces, villa and annexes, as well as the Museums and Library and the collections of art and archaeology therein are inalienable, exempt from any taxation or dues and not liable to be expropriated for reasons of public utility.

All told, a fair arrangement, considering that the kingdom of Italy held all the trump cards and that the Vatican had on its side only querulous protests, empty threats and a vague hope of being reinstated in its former domains by Austria, France, Prussia or whatever big power might possibly fight against and defeat the Italian kingdom. But not only Pius IX, who had been personally divested of temporal power, but also his successors rejected outright both the offer of friendship and the Law of Guarantees (which thus remained an entirely unilateral affair) and refused to collect the 3,225,000 lire a year or, for that matter, to use the privilege of sending telegrams without paying. They made it a question of principle and dignity.

Leo XIII (1878–1903), who succeeded Pius IX, was a tolerant man, as his encyclical *Rerum novarum* proves, but in the matter of the loss of temporal power he was just as uncompromising and acrimonious as his predecessor. One cannot help suspecting that his contention that private property was sanctioned by divine law was influenced by this issue. Italy retaliated by applying anti-clerical measures, by confiscating properties belonging to the religious orders, and a state of acute tension ensued. The Pope, in 1881, made plans to flee to Austria, establish the Holy See there and proclaim a kind of Holy War against the usurper of the Papal States. But Austria was not enthusiastic. Leo XIII, in the subsequent years, through his Secretary of State Cardinal Rampolla, approached other European capitals with this plan of escape but found a lukewarm reception. Finally the Italian Prime Minister Francesco Crispi heard about it, and made it known to Cardinal Rampolla that, if the Pope wished to leave Rome, Italy would put no obstacle in his way. But, he added, he could forget about coming back. The Pope stayed on.

But if Leo XIII failed to come to an understanding with Italy, he succeeded in lessening the tension created by his predecessor with Germany. The *Syllabus* of Pius IX, the proclamation of the Pope's infallibility by the Vatican Council I and the reactionary and authoritarian attitude of this Pope, had created a violent anti-clerical feeling in Germany which culminated in Bismark's *Kulturkampf* and in the drastic expropriations of practically all Catholic Church property. Under the soothing influence of Leo XIII the anti-Catholic laws were gradually abrogated. In 1882 Bismark sent Baron Kurt von Schlözer as Minister to the Holy See and Emperor Wilhelm II paid three visits to the Pope in 1888, 1893 and 1903. If the Catholic Church today still owns considerable properties in West Germany, this is partly due to Leo XIII.

To return to Rome, the loss of temporal power did not affect the finances of the Holy See too seriously. Added together, the loss of revenues from Latium, Abruzzi, Molise, Umbria, Romagna and Emilia amounted to a staggering figure. But as we have seen, the expenses far exceeded the revenues, so the Pope found himself better off, or at least less in debt. Also the tradition of collecting Peter's Pence all over the Catholic world was revived, much stimulated by the idea of helping 'the prisoner of the Vatican'.

The years between 1870 and 1929 are, so far as finance is concerned, wrapped in mystery. No budgets were published and it is difficult to get a clear idea of where the money came from. Now and then we find some scrap of news concerning sales of Church properties, but there are also purchases. Like the purchase of the Borghese and Barberini Libraries, which were added to the Vatican Library, and some shrewd buying-up of building sites in Rome.

At the beginning of the century several attempts were made to bring to an end the dispute between Church and State. The most promising was originated in June 1919 by a chance meeting in the lobby of the Hotel Ritz in Paris between Italy's Prime Minister Vittorio Emanuele Orlando who was attending the Versailles Peace Conference and the American prelate Mgr Kelley. The two discussed in general terms the possibility of a reconciliation. Mgr Kelley informed the Vatican and the Pope dispatched Mgr Cerreti, Secretary for Extraordinary Ecclesiastic Affairs, to Paris to go more deeply into the matter. The talks between the Vatican envoy and the Italian Prime Minister lasted a few days and both sides appeared hopeful. But when Orlando returned to Rome he was overthrown by parliament and the negotiations with the Holy See were abandoned.

In October 1922 Rome was conquered again, this time by the black-shirted legions of Mussolini. In the same year a former librarian, Achille Ratti, kindly and shrewd, had been elected Pope and had taken the name of Pius XI (1922–39). The stage was set. Mussolini, who in his youth had been an extreme Socialist and a rabid anti-clerical and who had written a pornographic novel called *The Mistress of the Cardinal,* was becoming, as the years went by, more and more conservative. His regime was firmly established but he realized that if he could put an end to the feud between Church and State, if he could win the official support of the Vatican (Fascism already enjoyed the sympathy of the majority of Italian priests), he would strengthen his position still more and greatly increase his importance on the international scene.

Pius XI was a realist. He saw the futility of the claim for the restitution of the Papal States and that it was more to the Church of Rome's advantage to make peace with Italy. He also realized that negotiating with a dictator, whose word was final and who could overrule the strong anti-clerical feeling still existing in Italy, would be easier than dealing with a parliamentary democracy.

The negotiations were started in great secrecy on 6 August 1926 by two intermediaries, who were both lawyers : Domenico Barone representing Mussolini and Francesco Pacelli representing Pius XI. Pacelli, a solicitor of the Vatican tribunal Sacra Rota (which deals with the annulment of marriage) was the brother of Eugenio Pacelli, then Papal Nuncio in Germany, future Cardinal and State Secretary and the future Pope Pius XII.

The negotiations lasted two and a half years. They were several times on the point of breaking up, but were then patiently resumed. At the most delicate moment, Domenico Barone died and Francesco Pacelli started dealing directly with Mussolini whom he visited at night in the Duce's dingy private apartment in the via Rasella. Mussolini had not yet moved to the more majestic Villa Torlonia. The more direct link was shortened also on the Vatican side as Pacelli started referring straight to the Pope instead of going through the Secretary of State, Cardinal Gasparri. This speeded up and simplified matters considerably. However, the final text of the Concordat had to be revised twenty times before the final approval and Francesco Pacelli had no less than 150 interviews with the Pope. The secrecy was absolute, both on the Vatican and on the Fascist side, which is more than extraordinary for Italy.

The Concordat, which was signed on 11 February 1929 by Cardinal Gasparri on behalf of the Pope and by Mussolini on behalf of King Victor Emmanuel III, apart from settling a quarrel that had been going on for fifty-nine years, gave birth to the Vatican City State in its present form and had a considerable influence on Vatican finances. It consisted of three documents : a treaty, a concordat and a financial convention. It is this last which we shall examine. Starting on a conciliatory and somewhat sugary note, the preamble states :

> The Supreme Pontiff, having considered on one hand the serious damage suffered by the Apostolic See from the loss of the ancient Papal States and of the properties of the ecclesiastical bodies, and on the other hand having considered the growing needs of the Church even if only in the City of Rome, but also keeping in mind the present financial situation of the State and the economic condition of the Italian people, especially after the war, has decided to limit to the strictly necessary the request of indemnity, asking for a sum, partly in cash and partly in bonds which is worth much less than the one the State should have paid to the Holy See in execution of the pledge taken by the law of May 31 1871.

This referred to the sum of 3,225,000 lire a year mentioned in the Law of Guarantees, but it ignored the fact that it was the Holy See who had refused to accept the payment. Anyhow, to make the somewhat embarrassing transaction easier on both sides, the preamble goes on :

> The Italian State, appreciating the fatherly feelings of the Supreme Pontiff, has deemed it dutiful to agree to the request for the payment of the said sum.

Then follow the hard facts, listing what Pius XI considered to be 'strictly necessary' and what Mussolini had agreed to give him :

Article 1. Italy undertakes to pay to the Holy See, on the ratification of the Treaty, the sum of 750 million Italian lire and to hand over at the same time Consolidated 5 per cent State Bonds to the bearer for the nominal value of one billion Italian lire.

Article 2. The Holy See declares the acceptance of the above as a definite settlement of its financial relations with Italy in connection with the events of 1870.

Mussolini tried to minimize the burden that the terms of the Concordat meant for the Italian State. The following speech to the Senate shows Mussolini's ability in juggling with figures, and gives a clear idea of what the Vatican got out of the deal:

As soon as the existence of a financial convention became known it was said, in round figures, to be somewhere in the region of two billion lire. Much less! It's a question, in fact, of 750 million in cash and of 1 billion in Consolidated Bonds which, I regret to say, can be bought today for only 800 million lire. Therefore, there are only 1,550 million lire involved, but paper lire. One must divide the figure by 3.66 and we get to 400 million gold lire.

It's very little, if you think that we have 200 billion lire of debt. It's a figure that makes you shiver. What are 400 million gold lire compared to it?

This juggling, the almost country-market-vendor skill of Mussolini in first pretending that 2 billion lire were involved, then reducing it to 1,750 million, then again to 1,550 million, then again converting the reduced figure to 400 million gold lire and finally comparing it to the 200 billion of the public debt, is self-evident, even if slightly naïve.

What matters, however, is that the actual value of the sum in cash and bonds received by the Holy See was very close to the middle figure Mussolini indicated: that is 1,550 million lire. This, at the rate of exchange current in those days, corresponded to approximately $81 million or £17 million.

Mussolini also explained how this financial operation could be carried out without greatly upsetting either the State budget or the financial market. As for the 1 billion lire worth of Consolidated State Bonds, he said, the Government would borrow them from the Loans and Deposits Fund, 'which has stacks of them anyhow' and give them back over a period of ten years buying each year on the market 100 million of their nominal value. As for the 750 million in cash, he explained that the State had a liquid reserve of two billion lire.

Furthermore, Mussolini tried to allay the fears that such a vast sum handed over to the Vatican at a single stroke might cause inflation and a further drop in the market value of the Consolidated Bonds. He said :

> Nothing exceptional and nothing catastrophic will happen. The crediting of the said sum will actually be made at the appointed date. But the Holy See—and here again one must say that the Supreme Pontiff has very liberally complied with our wishes—on the basis of agreements reached and in order not to increase circulation, will draw it from the Bank of Italy only gradually. Furthermore the Holy See has given us other assurances about the careful use of the one billion State Bonds, thus confirming the confidence in our bonds already shown by signing the financial convention.

We shall see later on what use the Vatican has made of those funds received by the Fascist Government, but we would like here to try and assess, on a more general plane, who gained and who lost what in concluding the Concordat.

On the whole, it looks as if Pius XI gained more advantages than Mussolini. The Holy See obtained the recognition of its sovereignty as a State and, if only in a miniature and almost symbolic way, the restoration of temporal power. It obtained all sorts of privileges, like the exemption from paying taxes, both for its properties and citizens, exemption from military service for Italians working for the Vatican, exemption from paying duty on imported goods, diplomatic immunity and privileges for Vatican diplomats and foreign diplomats accredited to the Holy See, the building of a railway station in the Vatican at the expense of the Italian State, and permission to install a radio station. In cases of *lèse-majesté* the Pope now stood equal to the King of Italy (or today to the President of the Republic). All attempts on the Pope's life, or insults publicly proffered against him on Italian territory by deeds, speeches or writings were to be punished by the same severe penalties as similar actions committed against the head of the Italian State. The sacred character of the city of Rome was recognized by the State which undertook to protect it; this is why strip-tease shows are forbidden and why the police prevented the showing of Rolf Hochhuth's play *The Deputy*.

The more lasting and substantial advantages gained by the Holy See, however, were the introduction of religious teaching (by teachers chosen by the Church) in all the State high schools and, last but not least, the fact that Mussolini, by signing the Concordat, placed the entire institution of marriage under canon law, which meant the ruling out of divorce. Article Seven of the Italian post-war Constitution, by embodying the Concordat, has made the position of the Vatican even stronger. At the time of writing a law introducing a limited type of divorce has been passed by the House of Deputies, but had still to be approved by the Senate. The Holy See lodged a strong diplomatic protest claiming that the introduction of divorce would violate the Concordat.

Mussolini's gains were mostly of a prestige and political nature. All the newly appointed bishops had to swear their allegiance to the Italian State and Government. All parish priests saying mass had to intone, on Sundays and other official holidays, a prayer for the prosperity of the King of Italy and his Government. The Fascist dictatorship had thus received the official Vatican blessing. Before appointing a new bishop the Holy See had to enquire whether there were any political objections on the part of the Government. All this still stands, in theory, while in practice it is easier for the Vatican to veto (unofficially of course) the appointment of an Italian Prime Minister than it is for the Government to veto the appointment of a bishop.

Catholic Action, going by the Concordat, was supposed to abstain from any political activity and from supporting any political party. Today, again, this still stands in theory, but in practice Catholic Action is fully engaged in supporting the Christian Democrats, Italy's strongest party and uninterruptedly in power since the end of the war. In order not to violate the Concordat too openly, the bishops, whenever there is a general election, set up special electoral organizations, controlled by the parish priests and called 'Civic Committees' which support Catholic candidates who usually come from Catholic Action. The name changes but the men are the same.

To sum up, the Concordat worked in favour of Mussolini when the Government was strong and the Church was weak, when his black-shirted thugs were allowed or ordered to seize and burn in the streets copies of the Vatican paper *Osservatore Romano* if it contained something of which Il Duce did not approve; and to beat up Catholic university students and wreck their headquarters. Today, now that the Church is strong and the Government weak, the position is largely reversed.

5

The Smallest State

Pope John was once asked by a visitor, 'Holy Father, how many people work in the Vatican?' His answer was, 'About half of them.'

Although many offices are sinecures and the atmosphere of Vatican City is no doubt serene and unhurried, I would not entirely agree with Roncalli's witticism. From my personal experience of the Vatican during the pontificates of Pius XII, John XXIII and Paul VI, it appeared that about a quarter take it easy, half work normally and the remaining quarter, including the Pope and the officials of the Secretariat of State, work much harder and keep longer office hours than any business executive in Detroit, Frankfurt, Milan, Manchester or Osaka.

Who are the citizens and inhabitants of this unique miniature State which is even smaller than Lichtenstein, Monaco, San Marino and Andorra? The citizens of the Vatican City—those who hold a Vatican passport—number 1,217, of whom 936 reside in the Vatican or in Rome and the rest, the Cardinals and members of the diplomatic corps, live abroad. Only 881 people actually live within the boundaries established by the 1929 Concordat. The others— some Cardinals, high Curia officials, lay clerks, journalists, gardeners, typographers, etc.—reside in Rome and go to the Vatican only to work. The resident population is swelled by five dogs, twelve canaries, one parrot and numerous cats. Apart from the priests, monks, friars and nuns, there live in the Vatican 153 families with fifty-seven children. The extremely low birth rate is due to the fact that the families are mostly made up of elderly servants, or elderly officers or officials whose children have grown up and left the Vatican.

In proportion to its population and size, Vatican City, the most peaceful State in the world, has an army bigger than that of Red China. The Pope's armed forces include one hundred and fifty

Gendarmes, seventy-five Swiss Guards (reduced from one hundred by Pope Paul), fifty Guards of Honour and about five hundred Palatine Guards, making a grand total of nearly eight hundred. But when one probes behind the façade and the figures, the military apparatus doesn't look as formidable as all that. Pope Paul has introduced many changes in this sector. The most important was the abolition of the Noble Guard, whose members, as the name indicates, were recruited from among the aristocracy. Blue blood was a condition *sine qua non*. The Noble Guard has been replaced by the Guard of Honour of His Holiness and noble birth is no longer necessary. In practice no new appointments have been made and the Guards of Honour are still the old Noble Guards. Presumably the idea is to let this anachronistic corps die out— gradually and with honour. The Guards of Honour have retained the gorgeous uniform of the Noble Guards, with spurred boots reaching above the knee, a big sword and a shiny helmet surmounted by a horse-hair mane. But Pope Paul has excluded them from all religious ceremonies and they now appear only in civil ceremonies of a solemn nature, as for instance when the Pope, as Head of State, receives another Head of State, or a Prime Minister, or when an ambassador presents his credentials.

Also excluded by Pope Paul from all religious ceremonies and less and less frequently called out on civil occasions are the five hundred Palatine Guards with their exotic uniforms. They are, historically, the descendants of the Roman populace which spontaneously rushed to the defence of the Pope in times of emergency. There is nothing snobbish about this corps and one can find among them butchers and professors, bus drivers and lawyers, road sweepers and architects united by their attachment to the Pope. They receive only a token payment of 15,000 lire a year to cover travelling expenses and the care of their uniforms and they are given a free meal when on duty. In view of the sporadic and honorary nature of their service and the fact that they do not live in the Vatican and have no Vatican citizenship, one should perhaps not include them in the Pope's regular army.

The Papal Gendarmes represent the real police force of Vatican City. The minimum required height is 1.75 metres, but the men are usually much taller. They are all Italians, mostly from the North, and will already have served either in the King's Cuirassiers, or in the Italian police or Carabinieri. In build and stolidity, they resemble the London police force. They are given a basic salary of 103,000 lire a month plus family allowances. The unmarried ones sleep in their barracks in the Vatican, the married ones sleep outside but they, too, must take their turn in spending one night out of three in the Vatican.

The Swiss Guards, as the name implies, are all Swiss, recruited from all the Swiss Cantons, except Italian-speaking Ticino. The German-speaking Cantons are preferred. Their pay is 74,000 lire a month, from which, however, mess and laundry expenses are deducted. Because of this low pay, most of the Swiss Guards are young men with private incomes who enlist because it offers them a chance of being near the Pope and learning Italian. The corps is proud of having had in its ranks famous writers, painters and musicians.

The highest paid Vatican officials are the Curia Cardinals, who receive a salary of 600,000 lire a month. Out of the first month's salary, immediately after the appointment, two-thirds are deducted and kept aside to provide for the Cardinal's funeral. *Memento mori.*

A deduction of 60,000 lire is made from the standard salary if the Cardinal lives in the Vatican or other Vatican-owned building in Rome rent free, while 60,000 are added if he has to pay rent. The Cardinal's salary is called a 'plate', from the days when it was made up of heavy gold and silver coins and handed to him on a plate or tray. Today, more prosaically, it is placed in an envelope which his secretary collects at the end of each month from the cashier of the Administration of the Holy See Property, on the first floor of the Apostolic Palace.

In addition to his fixed salary, a Cardinal also enjoys some extra revenue; fees for saying masses for the dead, or for performing marriages and baptisms; bonuses for taking part in committee work, or donations for having helped in promoting cases of beatification or canonization. But if a Cardinal earns good money, he also has expenses to meet. His robes, although lately simplified on instructions issued by the Pope, will cost him at least 1 million lire. He must live in a stately apartment, with one big reception room containing a red damask throne surmounted by a canopy, employ a few servants and possibly a good cook, and own an imposing automobile driven by a private chauffeur.

Up to a few years ago these prestige expenses were often borne, in part or in whole, by the *gentiluomini* of the Cardinal, that is, by laymen appointed to the private courts of the various Princes of the Church. These 'gentlemen' must have profited by their efforts, for there were among them businessmen and contractors. Paul VI has abolished the office of *gentiluomo* as he has also abolished that of *caudatario*, or tail-bearer. The tail (*cauda* in Latin) or train of a Cardinal's mantle (*cappa magna*) used to be eight metres long, but has been recently shortened first to three and then to two metres and will probably disappear altogether. This is just one of Pope John's and Pope Paul's modernizing and austerity measures.

The highest Curia official after a Cardinal is the secretary of a Congregation, paid on average 260,000 lire a month. Lower officials, naturally, get less and the impression is that people working for the Vatican are badly paid.[1] But side benefits must be taken into consideration. They are all exempt from tax,[2] many of them live in the Vatican rent-free, others in Rome in buildings owned by the Vatican, therefore paying very small rents, while all of them are able to buy petrol, cigarettes, spirits and all sorts of goods duty free.

In 1959, shortly after Pope John had increased Vatican salaries by about 50 per cent, the late Cardinal Tardini, Secretary of State, gave an unusual press conference at which, contrary to Vatican tradition, he let fall a few figures. Among other things he revealed that the payroll of the Vatican amounted to something in the region of $4\frac{1}{2}$ billion lire a year (about $7,250,000).

The whole of Vatican City, except for St Peter's Square, is encompassed by the Leonine Walls and takes up no more space than a golf course : 107.8 acres. The land and buildings assigned to the Holy See by the Concordat and which enjoy extra-territorial rights, scattered all over Rome, cover 180 acres, an area larger than Vatican City itself. This without counting the 135 acres of the pontifical summer residence at Castelgandolfo.

But if Vatican City is small, it nevertheless contains the most exceptional conglomeration of buildings and the largest and most valuable collection of art and books in the world. St Peter's Basilica,

---

[1] At the lowest level, a manual labourer earning 70,000 lire a month (about $115), would get double that amount if, for instance, he happened to be married with four children.
[2] Except for a nominal levy of 300 lire a month.

211 metres long and 140 high, remains the biggest church ever built. Its foundations rest on a Pagan cemetery and on the archaeological remains of what might well have been the tomb of St Peter. (Tucked away on the right-hand side of the basilica, and a bit difficult to find, there is a bar where you can drink an indifferent espresso, a Campari soda or a double whisky at a reasonable price.) Michelangelo's architectural genius crowned the basilica with its gigantic dome. As for the Vatican Palace, it contains, just to mention two glories of the Renaissance, Michelangelo's Sistine Chapel and Raphael's Stanzas.

The Vatican City State is made up of fifty buildings, six churches besides St Peter's, three cemeteries, the museums and the library : in all, it has about ten thousand rooms, halls and galleries, 12,523 windows and 997 stairs of all styles and sizes. It has a railway station connected to the Italian network but used only occasionally for heavy goods; four post offices, one tribunal, four barracks, one fire-station manned by twelve men with a jeep, a mosaic factory and a laboratory for mending tapestry, one rarely-used jail and three lifts. Of the three lifts, one is reserved for the exclusive use of the Pope. From a Latin inscription, one learns that the Latin word for lift is *anabatrum*.

St Anne's Gate, which gives access to the business section of the Vatican, is always very busy. Here is the post office, where pilgrims and tourists from all over the world buy stamps to the tune of $\$\frac{1}{2}$ million a year, a dairy, a kind of supermarket called *Annona* (from the Latin), the car pool, an underground garage and car park (the Vatican is congested with traffic and there are fines imposed), the printing-plant (they can print in most known languages, including some African dialects) and the offices of the four Vatican publications : the daily *Osservatore Romano*, the weekly *Osservatore della Domenica*, the monthly *Ecclesia*, all of them in Italian, and the official organ of the Holy See, *Acta Apostolicae Sedis*, in Latin. The Kremlin subscribes by post to two copies of *Osservatore Romano*.

Vatican City also has its own hotel, the Hospice of Santa Marta, with three hundred rooms and a restaurant. It caters only for special guests and groups of pilgrims and is cheap, but its doors close at 10 PM to reopen early next morning at 5.30 AM. Everyone living in the Vatican must be home by 11 o'clock at night, unless they make special arrangements with the Swiss Guards to be let in after the gates are locked. Similarly, guests from outside who are invited to dinner in a Vatican household are supposed to leave before 11 o'clock. The Dolce Vita is kept strictly out.

As a whole, the smallest State in the world could be described as a vast office and self-sufficient hotel run quietly, efficiently and economically on a non-profit basis by an assorted crowd of guards, policemen, courtiers, ushers, clerks, manual labourers, priests, monks, friars and nuns. The telephone switchboard, for instance, is run by six brothers of the Don Orione Society who answer incoming calls and connect them with the 2,000 telephones installed in the city and in some of the extra-territorial buildings. The Vatican must be the only State in which the number of telephones exceeds the number of inhabitants.

The pharmacy, where one can often find the latest medicines from Germany, Switzerland and the USA not yet approved by Italian health authorities, is run by the religious order Fatebene-fratelli. The Salesiani look after the bookshop and the printing-plant, Augustinians are in charge of the Papal ceremonial wardrobe, while nuns run the Santa Marta Hospice, and do cooking, cleaning, washing and mending in other Vatican premises, keeping very much in the background, almost unseen and unheard. The Pope himself has in his private apartment four elderly nuns who prepare his meals, sweep and dust his rooms, look after his everyday clothes, but never appear in public.

The Vatican is a strange mixture of traditional, ancient decor, protocol and customs, and modern efficiency. The Pope himself is an example of this dualism. When he appears at solemn functions he is carried on the gestatorial chair, surrounded by an almost Byzantine pomp, by Swiss Guards in striped uniforms carrying anachronistic halberds, and Papal dignitaries in colourful robes. But his private apartment is truly monastic, whitewashed, furnished with Swedish wooden and metal tables and chairs, steel office desk and filing cabinets, a dictaphone, a stereoscopic record player, a tape recorder, a radio and television set.

The finances and the technical administration of this peculiar microcosm called Vatican City are theoretically controlled by the Secretary of State and by a committee of Cardinals. In practice, however, it was a layman, Count Enrico Galeazzi, the Vatican architect, who held complete control from the days of Pius XII to 1969 and who was replaced by another layman, Marquis Giulio Sacchetti, as we shall see later.

6

The Roman Curia

'The Church, being a system, is systematic.'
Frederick Baron Corvo in *Chronicles of the House of Borgia.*

Before we go more deeply into the offices and the men in control of the Pope's financial empire, we would like, for a better understanding of the subject, to give the reader some sort of idea of how the Roman Curia is organized, after the reform carried out by Pope Paul and which came into force on 1 March 1968. Apart from the abolition of minor congregations and offices and several changes of name rather than substance, the chief novelty of the reform was the paramount importance given to the Secretariat of State and to the State Secretary. It was the official recognition of a *de facto* situation created by Pius XII. Eugenio Pacelli, who had been Secretary of State himself, continued to run this office also after he became Pope and attributed to it increasingly numerous and important tasks.

On page 78 we trace a simplified outline of the structure of the Catholic Church, in which several lesser offices, commissions, institutes, etc., have been omitted but which provides the backbone of the organization :

The Pope

College of Cardinals *Synod of Bishops*

State Secretariat and
Council for Public Affairs

Temporal and administrative power

Spiritual, judicial and doctrinal power

1. Prefecture for
   Economic Affairs
2. Administration of H.S.
   Patrimony
3. Institute for Religious
   Works
4. Governor of Vatican City
   controlling:
   a. Technical, financial
      and health services
   b. Swiss Guards
      Palatine Guards and
      Gendarmerie
   c. Vatican Museums and
      Library
   d. Vatican radio
   e. Vatican observatory
   f. Villa of Castelgandolfo

Congregation for the upkeep
of St Peter's

Congregations for the:
Doctrine of the Faith
Oriental Churches
Bishops
Discipline of Sacraments
Rites
Saints
Clergy
Religious Orders and
   Secular Institutes
Catholic Education
Propaganda Fide

Tribunals:
Apostolic Penitentiary
Sacra Rota (of appeal)
Apostolic Signatura (of
   cassation)

Permanent commissions and
secretariats of various
kinds

Apostolic Nuncios and Delegates

Bishops and ordinaries of the dioceses and of
other ecclesiastic jurisdictions

The clergy

The community of the faithful

To compare the Holy See to a lay State and Government might appear misleading and tricky, but it will help to clarify the situation. The Pope, then, is an absolute monarch whose powers have no limits and no controls. He is not responsible to anybody, except God and his own conscience. When he speaks *ex cathedra*, that is in the official exercise of his doctrinal and spiritual powers, he is also considered infallible by Catholics. Not so when he exercises his temporal and administrative powers.

The Secretariat of State is the core of the Curia and of the Church at large, the efficient and flexible instrument the Pope uses consistently to deal both with vital questions and with trivia. The Secretary of State, consequently, is the Pope's right-hand man and can be compared to the Prime Minister of a lay Government. He has been given the faculty, by Pope Paul's reform, to call together the heads of the various Congregations for a kind of Cabinet meeting. He acts as a link between the Pope on one side and the Bishops, the Vatican diplomatic representatives abroad and the Congregations and the remaining Curia offices on the other.

The Secretary of State is also the Prefect of the newly created Sacred Council for Public Affairs, in charge of diplomatic relations and negotiations with other States. The Secretary of State, therefore, combines the functions of a Prime Minister, Home Minister and Foreign Minister.

The College of Cardinals is described by canon law as the Senate of the Church. The fact that all its members are chosen and appointed by the sovereign and that they are, as a rule, elderly men of great experience and authority, confirms the description. On the other hand, the majority of the members of the Synod of Bishops are elected by Bishops from all over the world and therefore this new body created by Pope Paul has been compared to a democratic, representative Parliament. However, it is called together only when the Pope so decides, it can deal only with questions submitted to it by the Pope and its decisions are in no way binding, neither for the Pope nor for the Church. The comparison to a democratic Parliament therefore does not quite hold true.

The Congregations correspond in a loose way to Ministries and their Prefects may be compared to Cabinet Ministers. Below, without going into too many technical details, is an outline of their functions:

Congregation for the Doctrine of the Faith

This is the former Holy Office. It has lost the title of Supreme and it no longer has as its Prefect the Pope himself. Its task remains that of preventing deviation from the official doctrine and morals of the Catholic Church and of discovering and condemning heresies and theological mistakes. It can also examine and condemn heretical and immoral books brought to its attention. In certain cases it can function as a tribunal.

Congregation for the Oriental Churches

This supervises all Catholics of the Oriental rite and, with a few exceptions, is independent of the other Congregations. It carries out all the functions which, for the Church of the Latin rite, representing the overwhelming majority of Catholics, are scattered among the various Congregations. It is a kind of small Curia specialising in the Oriental Churches.

Congregation for the Bishops
(the former Consistorial Congregation)

This has the power to create new dioceses, abolish old ones, unite them or divide them, but not in the territories controlled by the Congregation for the Oriental Churches. It deals with the appointment of Bishops—the final decision always resting with the Pope—and with everything that concerns their pastoral and personal problems. It studies the periodical reports written by the Bishops about the state of the respective dioceses and, when necessary, sends apostolic visitors to carry out inspections.

Congregation for the Discipline of Sacraments

This, as the name suggests, supervises the proper use of the seven sacraments and deals with the cases of marriages celebrated but not consummated.

Congregation of Rites

This is entrusted with the application and the supervision of the reform of liturgy approved by the Ecumenical Council.

The Congregation for the Causes of the Saints

Newly created as an offshoot of the Congregation of Rites, it deals with canonizations and beatifications.

Congregation for the Clergy

This is the former Congregation of the Council. Besides looking after the clergy in general, trying to stimulate their zeal, raise their cultural standards, and employ them to the best of their capacities, etc., it also has considerable financial control. We shall return to this Congregation in greater detail when we examine the more strictly financial bodies of the Church.

Congregation for the Religious and Secular Institutions

This supervises Jesuits, Franciscans, Benedictines, Dominicans and all the other innumerable orders of monks, friars, regular clerics and nuns. It controls (in a rather loose way, as all the orders are proud of their independence) about a million women and a quarter of a million men. To this has been added a special section which deals with the flourishing Secular Institutes, the organizations of lay men and women who, without changing their professions and continuing to wear civilian clothes, take privately the vows of obedience, poverty and chastity and carry out their apostolate in various forms.

This Congregation carries out some kind of control over the finances of the orders, but as they have separate patrimonies, capitals, budgets and administrations, the control, here again, is rather loose. I am told that the richest order, strangely enough, is that of the Franciscans, closely followed by the Jesuits. But to follow the financial affairs of all the religious orders and of the secular institutes, as for instance the powerful and semi-secret Spanish 'Opus Dei', would be like entering a jungle. My task is limited to dealing with central Vatican finances.

Congregation for Catholic Education

This is the former Congregation for Seminaries and Universities of Studies. As the change of name indicates, it has broadened its scope which is that of spreading the knowledge of the Catholic religion as widely as possible.

Congregation of Propaganda Fide

This has retained its historical Latin name, but it is now also called *Congregation for the Evangelization of the Peoples*. It deals with the missions scattered all over the world. As it has its own financial organization and large amounts of money are involved, we shall dedicate to it a separate chapter.

One of the big novelties of Pope Paul's reform was the creation of an entirely new office, the PREFECTURE FOR ECONOMIC AFFAIRS, which may be considered as a kind of Budget Ministry. The creation of this new office confirms what I said in the Introduction, that the Pope was dissatisfied with the way Vatican finances were being handled and wanted to know more precisely what was going on in order to co-ordinate the otherwise scattered and independent financial activities. But before we explain how the Prefecture for Economic Affairs is supposed to work, it will be better to take a closer look at the financial organizations which the Pope has placed under its control.

7

The Pope's Coffers

The main Vatican offices and organizations which deal preeminently with financial affairs are the following:

The Administration of the Holy See Patrimony[1]
The Institute for Religious Works
The Governatorate of the Vatican City State
Propaganda Fide
The Pius XII Foundation for Lay Apostolate
The State Secretariat
The Congregation of the Clergy
The Prefecture for Economic Affairs

Let us take a closer look at them.

The Administration of the Holy See Patrimony
This is the result of a merger, carried out by Pope Paul in May 1968, of two offices—the Administration of the Holy See Properties (Amministrazione dei Beni della Santa Sede) and the Special Administration (Amministrazione Speciale). For a better understanding of the situation, I think it convenient to describe what these two administrations were and what they did before Pope Paul's reform.

The Administration of the Holy See Properties
In theory it should be considered the wealthiest of them all. For the value of St Peter's, of Bernini's colonnade, of the conglomeration of majestic palaces that form this unique city, is immeasurable. Who could or would dare to put a price on Michelangelo's Pietà and Last Judgment, or on the medieval sculpture of the Good

[1] Also known as the Administration of the Patrimony of the Apostolic See.

Shepherd, or on Raphael's or Pinturicchio's frescoes, or on the Egyptian papyri in the Vatican library or, for that matter, on the relics of the Cross, or on the spear which is said to have pierced Christ's ribs (whatever authenticity one attributes to these objects) or on the tomb of St Peter himself?

It is all rather abstract. These objects are not for sale, they don't bring in any revenue (except for the modest entrance fees to the Museums, which go to the Governatorate anyhow), but on the contrary require considerable sums for their upkeep.

The loss of temporal power in 1870 radically upset the whole financial and administrative structure of the Holy See and the reluctance of Pius IX to accept the new situation left everything in a state of flux. Only eight years later, on 9 August 1878, Leo XIII appointed his Secretary of State, Cardinal Nina, administrator of the whole patrimony that was left. Later still he nominated a committee of Cardinals to supervize the administration of Peter's Pence and of the Holy See properties. Finally the same Pope, in 1891, gave the Cardinals more power to administer the patrimony directly and to embark on financial operations. He also ruled that the said committee continue to function between the death of a Pope and the election of a new one. In 1926 Pius XI increased even further the power of the committee, entrusting to it the administration of the Apostolic Palaces and the administrative sections of the various congregations and offices.

This means that, besides bearing the considerable cost of the upkeep of the Apostolic Palaces, this office had to pay the salaries of all Curia Cardinals and lesser ecclesiastic and lay officials and clerks, except those depending directly on the Governatorate. It is difficult to distinguish and number exactly who was paid by the Administration of the Holy See Properties (and now by the Administration of the Holy See Patrimony) and who by the Governatorate. I can only state from Vatican sources that the Holy See has on its payroll about three thousand people and that it pays out in salaries about $10 million a year. The figure has gone up since Cardinal Tardini revealed that it amounted to $7,500,000. All things considered, it is a very modest average salary of something less than $280 a month, which includes Cardinals and gardeners, newspaper editors and firemen.

The contradiction between the number of people on the Holy

See payroll and the numbers of Vatican citizens and inhabitants, quoted in Chapter Five, is only too apparent. For there are people who work in the Vatican but are not Vatican citizens and many more who work on various premises scattered all over Rome, like the Cancelleria, the Vicarage of Rome in the Piazza San Calisto, the Propaganda Fide palace in the Piazza di Spagna, the huge palace of the Congregations in Trastevere, various buildings in the Via della Conciliazione and so on.

The Administration of the Holy See Properties also bore the cost of running the Vatican daily paper *Osservatore Romano* and other Vatican publications. It paid the salaries and expenses of the Holy See observers or delegates to the United Nations, FAO, UNESCO, the Atomic Energy Commission in Vienna and other international bodies. On the other hand, the costs of the vast Vatican diplomatic corps spread all over the world was not borne by this administration nor, as one might think, by the Secretariat of State. Going by an old tradition, the local religious orders pay the bills of the Vatican diplomats in the respective countries.

But from where did the Administration of the Holy See Properties and from where does the Administration of the Holy See Patrimony now derive the vast sums necessary to perform its heavy tasks? Partly from real estate—from the rents of apartments and shops owned by the Vatican in Italy and particularly in Rome. Partly from the dividends of bonds and industrial shares owned by the administration both in Italy and abroad. However, as we shall see later in greater detail, the Administration of the Holy See Properties had less money invested in Italy than other Vatican financial bodies.

The Special Administration

This is definitely the most mysterious of them all. This financial office was created especially by Pius XI, on 7 June 1929, to administer the capital of 1,550 million lire that Mussolini had handed over to the Holy See in execution of the Concordat. From its foundation until 1958 this special fund was to all practical purposes administered single-handed by a layman, Bernardino Nogara, an engineer and banker, brother of the director of the Vatican Museums. Nogara, before his appointment, had been director of a branch of the Banca Commerciale Italiana in Istanbul where he specialized in the arbitration of gold. After his appointment as Delegate of the Special Administration, he became Vice-President of the Banca Commerciale Italiana. Despite this link, the Banca Commerciale has practically no connection with Vatican capital and men. Nogara, who died in 1958, was deeply religious and entirely dedicated to his work. Under his able guidance, with sound investments made both in Italy and abroad, the Special Administration was able to increase considerably the initial sum it had received from the Italian Government.

True to its name and history, the Special Administration did not carry out any routine work but specialized in investments and big financial deals. It could be considered as the 'commando force' of Vatican finances.

In practice, after the death of Nogara, the Special Administration was run by another layman, the Swiss Marquis Henri de Maillardoz, a former director of the Crédit Suisse, who has since retired, and by Mgr Sergio Guerri, who was subsequently made a Cardinal, a placid, cordial prelate from Tarquinia, near Rome, but quite a tough negotiator.

The actual administrative work is carried out by a staff of seventeen clerks and accountants, all Italian laymen, housed in an apartment of the Vatican Palace, not far from that of the Pope. The strictest secrecy surrounds the whole operation. Red tape is reduced to the minimum and most of the big deals are carried out by word of mouth, in private interviews or over the telephone. Complete trust is the basis of the relationship between the Vatican and its partners in the financial world.

But what of these connections, about which so much has been written, based only too often on the vaguest of hints, between the Vatican and the world of international finances? It is difficult to say because of the very complexity and fragmentation of the financial set-up of the Holy See. But, to restrict the field to the Special Administration, I would mention the Rothschilds in Paris and London, the Crédit Suisse (through Maillardoz), Hambros Bank in London, the J. P. Morgan Bank in New York and, last but not least, the Bankers Trust Company of New York. One of the Vice-Presidents of the Bankers Trust Company, Mr Andrew P. Maloney, is the Economic and Social Adviser of the Holy See mission to the United Nations. The Bankers Trust has an office in

Rome, 76 via Bissolati, headed by Count Sebastiano Bommartini. I understand, however, that, because of the tradition of utmost secrecy, whenever the Holy See decides to buy or sell shares on Wall Street, an official of the Special Administration telephones directly to the Bankers Trust Company in New York without going through the Rome office.

In May 1968 Pope Paul joined together these two key administrations and called the new body the Administration of the Holy See Patrimony. At the head of it he placed, or rather confirmed, the Secretary of State Cardinal Amleto Cicognani, who already presided over the two previous administrations. Subsequently, when Cicognani was replaced as Secretary of State by Jean Villot, the French Cardinal also became President of the Administration of the Patrimony. Villot is assisted by a committee of Cardinals, a kind of board of directors, including Alberto di Jorio who appears in most of the offices dealing with finances.

The Administration of the Holy See Patrimony has been divided in two sections: ordinary and extraordinary, which correspond respectively to the previous Administration of the Holy See Properties and to the Special Administration. Mgr Gaspare Cantagalli, who was already in charge of the State Secretariat funds, was appointed Delegate of the ordinary section. Marquis de Maillardoz was replaced by the Italian banker Benedetto Argentieri as Delegate of the extraordinary section. More or less the same men have remained in the same jobs doing the same things. The main difference is that the overall command of the operations has been unified. The key men are Villot, Guerri, di Jorio, Argentieri and Cantagalli.

The Institute for Religious Works

Despite its high sounding name, this is simply the bank of the Vatican. It was founded by Pius XII in June 1942 and has taken over the Administration of Religious Works set up by Leo XIII in 1887.

The Vatican bank is housed in the tower of Nicholas V, near St Anne's Gate, and has a Pontifical Gendarme guarding its entrance. The Institute works like any other bank. It has its counters and its lay cashiers, it accepts deposits, opens current accounts, cashes cheques and transfers money. It also has a branch outside the Vatican, but quite close to St Peter's square.

The big difference between it and other banks is that its clients are a very select group. The only people who can open an account with the Institute are residents of the Vatican City State, diplomatists accredited to the Holy See, members of the Curia, heads of the religious orders, other religious who administer schools, hospitals and other institutions, and a very few Italian citizens to whom the privilege was granted because of their business relations with the Vatican or their good work on behalf of the Church. The advantage of banking with the Vatican—prestige apart—is that one is completely free of Italian currency regulations and one can transfer money to any part of the world with maximum ease. The Pope's current account is reported to bear the number 16/16.

It is a custom, if not a rule, for laymen using the Institute as their bank, to leave in their wills a proportion of their deposits (usually 10 per cent), or a lump sum, to the Institute itself. The Institute, as we shall see later, has a vast amount of money invested in Italian shares, more, as a matter of fact, than any other Vatican financial organization.

It is supervized by a committee of Cardinals, including Villot, Guerri and di Jorio, and its secretary is the American Mgr Paul Marcinkus. Apart from two more prelates, the other ten employees are all laymen. Signor Luigi Mennini figures prominently among them; he has the title of Delegate, and represents Vatican interests on the board of many big Italian companies. The key-men are Villot, di Jorio, Marcinkus and Mennini.

The Governatorate of the Vatican City State

As we saw, Vatican City is a small State indeed, but with its own armed forces and police, fire brigade and various offices that look after finances, personnel, health, transport, food and public works. As its citizens do not pay taxes, its revenues consist of the sale of stamps and coins, the entrance tickets to the Vatican Museums and a reasonable margin of profit made on the sale of cigarettes, petrol, spirits and other goods sold in the Vatican shops.

The sale of stamps, during the last decade, has turned into quite a big business. Here too Vatican secrecy prevails, but, thanks to some recently discovered data, we can give the reader at least an idea of the magnitude of the phenomenon. First of all one must distinguish between the normal sale of stamps in the Vatican post office (mostly to pilgrims and tourists buying postcards to send home or to friends as a souvenir of their visit) and the sale to stamp dealers and collectors of special series issued to commemorate centenaries or other religious events.

The special series, which appear very frequently, constitute the main revenue. During the reign of Pius XII they were limited to 300,000 or 400,000 sets for each series. But as they were in great demand, they were increased up to 1964 to about two million sets per series. Later they were further increased and a peak of seven million sets per series was reached in 1965. This was too much and the market showed signs of saturation. There was a danger of inflation and of consequent devaluation of Vatican stamps. Therefore, since 1966, the number of sets for each series has been limited to just over two million.

How much money do stamps bring in? I shall quote as an example three series that were put on sale at the end of 1967 : the one issued to commemorate the miracle of Fatima, the one put out on the occasion of the World Congress of Laymen held in Rome and the Christmas series. The Fatima series had a face value of 280 lire and was printed in 2,300,000 sets, thus bringing 644 million lire into the coffers of the Governatorate. The Laymen series had a 170 lire face value, was printed in 2,400,000 sets and brought in 424 million. The Christmas series had a face value of 280, was printed in 2 million sets and brought in 560 million lire. Thus, with only three series put on sale at the end of 1967 the Vatican made 1,628 million lire, that is about $2,300,000. This without counting the routine sale of stamps which, as we said before, brings in about $½ million a year.

The story does not end here. Vatican stamps, especially the series, have a great appeal and increase in value rapidly within a few weeks of their issue. For instance, the three series we have mentioned above were quoted in the market at around 1,000 lire for each set by the beginning of December 1967. And here another interesting factor intervenes. Only a limited amount of sets for each series is sold to private stamp dealers and collectors who must book in advance and are rationed to ten sets each. For instance, only 400,000 sets of the Christmas series were sold to private people. The other 1,600,000 were sold to religious orders and other Church institutions. The same thing happens, more or less, to all series issued by the Vatican. The religious orders and the other institutions, in turn, sell them to stamp dealers with a quite handsome margin of profit. Thus not only the Vatican but the Church as a whole derive a considerable benefit from the sale of stamps.

In theory the Governatorate is run by a committee of Cardinals which has the State Secretary Villot as President and Guerri as Pro-President. In practice, until the beginning of 1968, the finances of the Vatican City State were completely in the hands of a layman, Count Enrico Galeazzi, the Vatican architect and a protegé of Pius XII. It was this Pope who left vacant the post of Governor (which in the old days was held by the Camerlengo) and entrusted it to his close friend Galeazzi with the title of Special Delegate. Count Galeazzi was also given the jobs of Director General of the Economic Services and of Director General of the Technical Services. He thus had complete control of all the vital offices of the Vatican City. Galeazzi proved to be a very able administrator and was confirmed in his post first by Pope John and subsequently by Pope Paul.

It was only on 25 March 1968 that Pope Paul, in the framework of a more general reform of the Roman Curia, put an end to Galeazzi's long rule over Vatican City. He nominated in his place, again with the title of Special Delegate, Marquis Giulio Sacchetti, son of Giovanni Battista Sacchetti who holds important Vatican jobs and who is one of the outstanding Italian financiers closely linked to the Holy See.

Giulio Sacchetti, however, does not hold the strong position which Galeazzi had in the Governatorate. To start with, the jobs of Director General of Economic Services and of Director General of Technical Services which Galeazzi also held, had been assigned respectively to Engineer Italo Viesi and to Signor Adolfo Soleti. In the second place, Pope Paul created a brand new advisory Committee (Consulta) of twenty-four lay members to deal with Vatican City State affairs. The Consulta presumably will weaken the influence of the General Consulter, Prince Carlo Pacelli, who had been nominated by his uncle Pius XII, as the respective functions appear to overlap.

The general tendency of Pope Paul in reforming the Curia has been to copy modern lay administrations. The Consulta therefore has been compared in Vatican quarters to a kind of town Council. Its twenty-four members, who will advise on the administration of the smallest State in the world, are men from widely differing spheres of society and of influence. There are seven members of the Roman aristocracy (Prince Aspreno Colonna, Prince Alessandro Torlonia, Prince Leone Massino, Marquis Giovanni Battista Sacchetti, Marquis Giacomo Serlupi Crescenzi, Marquis Filippo Patrizi and Count Antonio Alberti-Poja), five professors, two lawyers including the former Christian Democrat mayor of Rome, Urbano Cioccetti, other top professional men and two women, Signora Pia Colini Lombardi and Signora Maria Luisa Paronetto-Valier, both leading figures in Catholic Action.

Of these, Signora Pia Colini Lombardi is perhaps the most colourful. Sister of the famous Jesuit Father Riccardo Lombardi, a preacher so eloquent that he earned himself the nickname of 'God's microphone', she has taken a very active part in the abolition of State controlled brothels in Italy and is still engaged in the redemption of prostitutes. She told me quite frankly that, although she was extremely flattered by Pope Paul's decision to include her in the Consulta, she did not have the faintest idea of what her contribution could be in solving the problems of this unique city. Certainly not, I may add, the redemption of prostitutes.

To return to Count Galeazzi, his retirement from the Governatorate of Vatican City coincided with his appointment as President of Immobiliare, the biggest Italian real estate and building company, tightly controlled by men who enjoy the confidence of the Vatican. The Count was confirmed by Pope Paul in his posts as Architect of the Apostolic Palaces, Architect of St Peter's Basilica and member of the permanent commission for the protection of historical and artistic monuments of the Holy See.

The Governatorate also controls, from an administrative point of view, the Vatican Museums, the Vatican radio and observatory, the Villa of Castelgandolfo and the Pontifical Gendarmerie, while the Swiss Guards and the Guards of Honour are controlled by the Secretariat of State.

The Congregation for the Clergy

As we have seen, this looks after clergy in general, endeavouring to stimulate their zeal and piety, raise their cultural level and place them in the best possible conditions in order that they may successfully carry out their apostolate. But it also has very important administrative and financial tasks.

This Congregation gives instructions on the use and administration of ecclesiastical properties, on the execution of wills made in favour of the Church, on the acceptance of legacies and trusts, on the sale or mortgaging of real estate and so on. It also fixes the fees to be collected for masses and other church ceremonies and the sums which the bishops can draw from the estates of the respective dioceses.

It is the task of this Congregation to study all the projects which require considerable sums of money and to examine, on the basis of a sound economy, the possibilities of borrowing money. When some local enterprise looks promising but cannot be accomplished for lack of funds, the Financial Office of the Congregation steps in with its own contribution. It also finances the reconstruction of churches, schools, parishes destroyed by war, earthquakes, floods or other calamities if local resources are not enough. It supervizes the use to which ecclesiastical properties are put and gives financial assistance to particularly poor priests and to needy relatives of deceased priests. The case of elderly sisters of priests who never married and dedicated their entire lives to look after the household of their brothers is typical.

The importance and the technical character of business dealt with by this Congregation require a specialized staff. In 1919 Benedict XV attached to the financial office a school attended by young priests who take a three-year course.

The Congregation is supervized by a committee of no less than thirty-six Cardinals, partly living in Rome and partly in their dioceses abroad. Among the consultants of the administrative section we find Signor Luigi Mennini. The Prefect of this Congregation is the American Cardinal John Joseph Wright.

The Prefecture for Economic Affairs

As we saw, the administration of Vatican finances is carried out by several offices of which the more important ones have been described and which are independent from each other. In order to try and coordinate their activities and those of other minor offices Pope Paul created the Prefecture for Economic Affairs. This new office came into being on 1 March 1968 and it is still not clear how it works in practice. According to its constitution, it should be a kind of Budget Ministry and a controlling authority combined. The Papal document that set up this office ruled that all Vatican administrations, in Rome and outside, even those that are autonomous, including the various commissions and secretariats, must give to the Prefecture an account of their revenues and of their expenses, submit a budget and an estimate of future expenses. Only the Institute for Religious Works has been exempted from the supervision of the Prefecture.

The new office, after having gathered all these data, will prepare, and possibly has already done so, a general budget of Holy See finances and will submit it to the Pope's approval. Before the institution of this central financial office, a kind of budget was prepared by Cardinal di Jorio who, as we saw, has his fingers in most of the financial pies. But it was something rather approximate, as he didn't have all the necessary data available.

But will the new, more detailed and all-embracing budget be made public? The final decision rests with the Pope and also on the extent to which the renewal of the Church of Rome, started by Pope John and the Ecumenical Council and continued within certain limits by Pope Paul, will be pushed forward.

Once again I must venture the opinion that the secrecy is more harmful than useful. When in 1953 an Italian magazine, whose story was taken up in many other countries, wrote that the wealth of the Vatican was second only to that of the United States, and which was no doubt a gross exaggeration, there was a marked drop in offerings and donations to the Church. If they are so wealthy, people must have thought, why give them money? On that occasion Mgr Giovan Battista Montini, then Pro-Secretary of State, remarked bitterly: 'That article dried up the Pope's sources of charity!' It is no use for the Vatican simply to issue an affronted denial of exaggerated reports. The denials, to be convincing, should be accompanied by the disclosure of the real situation.

One of the most staggering rumours I heard from a Monsignore is that the Vatican secretly owns the 'Grand Mogul', the biggest diamond in the world, weighing 280 carats. It was last seen in the middle of the seventeenth century by the French traveller Tavernier, at the court of the Great Mogul, Aurangzeb. According to my informer, it was bought by the Vatican in the East during the reign of Pacelli.

The Prefecture is now empowered to inspect the books and documents of the various administrations and whenever it finds items that exceed routine expenditure, it must present a written report to the Pope. It is also entrusted with the task of controlling and coordinating investments and big financial operations carried out by the Holy See. In the same way, when there is a major building project to be carried out, the Prefecture must study and approve the estimates and supervize the execution of the work. The Prefecture has no capital of its own but, in order to cover its administrative expenses, it draws 1 per cent from the revenues of the Administration of the Holy See Patrimony.

This new-born office has already suffered, at top level, many radical changes. The Pope had originally appointed as President of the Prefecture Cardinal Angelo Dell'Acqua and as his assistants the American Cardinal Francis Brennan and the Dutch Cardinal Maximilian de Furstenberg. Dell'Acqua is an old Curia hand who has worked in the Secretariat of State reaching the high rank of Substitute for Ordinary Affairs, the same post the present Pope held for many years before becoming Archbishop of Milan. Brennan had been the Dean of the Sacra Rota Tribunal while de Furstenberg had been Nuncio in Portugal.

But before the Prefecture actually started working, the trio was disbanded. Dell'Acqua was made Vicar General of the Diocese of Rome. It is known that the Pope himself is by tradition Bishop of the Eternal City. In practice, however, because of his heavy commitments as head of the Universal Church, he has no time to perform his duty as bishop and needs a Vicar. To all practical purposes Dell'Acqua is the real Bishop of Rome which, coupled with his diplomatic background, might constitute a sound stepping-stone towards the papacy. Brennan was made Prefect of the Congregation for the Discipline of the Sacraments and de Furstenberg Prefect of the Congregation for the Oriental Churches.

The new head of the Prefecture for Economic Affairs is Cardinal Egidio Vagnozzi, a Roman and a typical product of Vatican diplomacy : affable, able and cautious. He was from 1951 to 1958 Nuncio to the Philippines and from 1958 to 1967 Apostolic Delegate to Washington, where he succeeded the future Secretary of State

Cardinal Amleto Cicognani. During the long period spent in the United States he became closely acquainted with that financial genius Cardinal Spellman, Archbishop of New York, and through him established connections with Wall Street which may prove useful in his job and which in fact may account for his appointment. Cardinal Vagnozzi is considered in Vatican circles to incline towards conservatism and it is believed that, while he remains in charge of the Prefecture, no budget will be made public. The other two Cardinals appointed by Pope Paul to assist Vagnozzi were the Czechoslovak Cardinal Joseph Beran, who subsequently died, and the Italian Cardinal Cesare Zerba. Beran, the former Archbishop of Prague, was for many years a prisoner of the Communists and he was called to Rome after his liberation to eliminate friction between the Holy See and the Czechoslovak State. Cardinal Zerba is a former high official of the Roman Curia who has already had considerable administrative experience. Beran's place was taken by Giacomo Violardo, an Italian, who was made a Cardinal in April 1969.

The reforms carried out by Pope Paul also ruled that the three Cardinals in charge of the Prefecture, and all other top Curia officials for that matter, must be confirmed in their jobs every five years. If not so confirmed, they are automatically replaced. This could mean that the monopoly in the financial affairs of the Holy See, which Pope Pius XII gave into the hands of his three nephews, a few chosen laymen and a few ecclesiastics, could come to an end.

Pope Paul also decided that the Prefecture should be assisted by a group of lay and ecclesiastic consultants. At the moment of writing they had not yet been chosen or, at least, their names had not been disclosed. But I understand that there have been difficulties. Most of the lay experts approached had agreed to act as consultants, but only on condition they be given a complete picture of the financial situation, which the Vatican was still unwilling to do.

This would seem to be as good a time as any to ask the following questions: how efficient is the Holy See in running its finances? How clever are Vatican financiers?

On the whole, I would say that it is very efficient, that it carries out a great deal of work with a minimum of staff and red tape. People in charge are given ample trust and ample powers to make decisions. Not infrequently important deals are concluded with a single telephone call. But while the Holy See, when necessary, can act extremely fast, it has also developed to a fine art the tactics of procrastination.

Vatican financiers are in a privileged position. They have no currency restrictions, they pay no taxes, they do not have to show immediate profits nor account to shareholders and they possess, through Vatican diplomats abroad, through bishops and trusted lay Catholic businessmen all over the world, a net of informers and operators that would be the envy of any big international company or, for that matter, of any government. If a criticism can be expressed it is that they have not taken full advantage of this privileged situation, preferring a more 'parochial' attitude. I would still subscribe to the opinion of the American Institute of Management which in 1956 carried out a study on the efficiency of the Church of Rome. They concluded that the Vatican investment of capital mainly in Italy could mean one of two things : either ignorance of better investment opportunities abroad, or that it was more expedient to control Italian enterprises. The decision to invest in Italian hotels and banks could not be called a clever one, considering that the Vatican is in a position to note the slightest change in the world financial situation.

8

Vatican Lay Financiers

As we have seen so far, it is not too difficult to find out which main bodies administer Vatican finances, their individual functions, and the people in charge : the Pontifical Yearbook supplies most of the answers. The difficulty begins when we try to ascertain where, how, and how much Vatican money is invested abroad; that is, outside the confines of the Vatican City. On this subject both the Pontifical Yearbook and Vatican official spokesmen are silent. We shall, however, try to unravel the mystery.

According to Italian financial circles and from various indiscretions dropped by well-informed men in the Vatican, more than two-thirds and perhaps even over three-quarters of the capital is invested in Italy. The reasons are fairly obvious. A large proportion of the property left to the Holy See after 1870 was in Italy and has remained there. Moreover the 1,550 million lire the Holy See received in 1929 from the Fascist Government was partly in Italian currency and partly in Italian State Bonds. In the third place the Curial offices dealing with money have been and to a lesser extent still are in the hands of Italian prelates and it was only natural that they should entrust financial operations to other Italians whom they knew well and on whom they could rely. Let us, therefore, start with Italy.

The bulk of these financial operations is carried out by a restricted group of Italian laymen closely connected to the Roman Curia by their jobs, titles, tradition and family ties. That laymen, instead of ecclesiastics, should be in charge is also fairly obvious. It would have been not only embarrassing for a Cardinal or a top Curia official to sit on the board of directors of an Italian company but also technically impossible because of his Vatican citizenship. Moreover, the use of laymen is an additional guarantee of secrecy as, although their ties with the Vatican may be known, it is

97

impossible to determine exactly to what extent they operate on behalf of the Vatican or on their own.

Speaking again in general terms, one notes that the backbone of the present financial organization was created by and under Pope Pius XII. Pope John, who had an allergy for financial matters, left things unchanged, while Pope Paul started a reform the full effects of which remain to be seen. One can also note that nepotism, both in a literal and in a wide sense, had a great part in it.

One of the main characteristics of Pope Pius was his aloofness and loneliness. A very clever man, a prodigious worker endowed with an equally prodigious memory, Pius XII was a perfectionist who hated to delegate to others what he could himself do better. He had few collaborators—the chief of them having been for many years Giovan Battista Montini, the present Pope—and a predilection for the Germans whom he appreciated for their qualities of punctiliousness and reliability. His two private secretaries, his housekeeper, Mother Pasqualina Lehnert, and his confessor, the late Cardinal Augustin Bea, were all Germans. He had very few close friends and he preferred, strangely enough, laymen to ecclesiastics. Pacelli's friends can be counted on the fingers of two hands: the Vatican architect Count Enrico Galeazzi, his nephew Prince Carlo Pacelli, to a lesser extent his other two nephews the Princes Giulio and Marcantonio Pacelli, his doctor Riccardo Galeazzi-Lisi (half-brother of architect Galeazzi) and Professor Luigi Gedda, a Catholic Action leader, also a doctor who specializes in scientific research on twins. Among non-Italians he was friendly with the German Mgr Ludwig Kaas, former leader of the German Catholic Party, Centrum, who had been compelled to flee to Rome by the advent of Hitler. Another exception to the laymen-preferred rule was the late Cardinal Francis Spellman, Archbishop of New York; the two men had become friends when working together in the Secretariat of State in their youth. Spellman was the only Cardinal to be immediately received by the Pope on his arrival in Rome, the only one who was sometimes invited to take tea with him and the only one who could afford the liberty of giving the Pope an electric razor as a present. During the last years of his life Pacelli also became very friendly with another doctor, the Swiss Paul Niehans, who had given him the so-called living cells rejuvenation cure. The Niehans cure, which has been fashionable for some time, is still regarded with considerable scepticism by official medical opinion. Nevertheless, Pacelli believed in Niehans and made him a member of the Pontifical Academy of Sciences in 1955.

But to return to the matter of Pacelli's nepotism and preference for laymen; this had a considerable and lasting influence on Vatican financial affairs. As we have mentioned the word nepotism, let us start with the three nephews of Pius XII, the Princes Carlo, Marcantonio and Giulio Pacelli. Contrary to what one would expect, they do not in fact belong to the 'Black' or Vatican aristocracy. The hereditary title of prince was given to them by King Victor Emmanuel III, following a suggestion by his Prime Minister Benito Mussolini, as a compensation to their father, Francesco Pacelli, a lawyer of the Sacra Rota and brother of the future Pius XII, for the part he had played in the secret negotiations that resulted in the 1929 Concordat.

Of the three nephews, Carlo was the Pope's favourite. He had free access to the private apartment of his uncle who liked to consult him frequently. His privileged position is reflected by the Vatican jobs and titles that were bestowed on him by Pope Pius and which he still retains.

Prince Carlo Pacelli who, like his brothers, followed in his father's footsteps and became a lawyer, is legal adviser to the Administration of the Holy See Patrimony, general consultant to the Pontifical Committee for the Vatican City State, legal adviser to the administration of Propaganda Fide, legal adviser to the Pontifical Society for Religious Vocations (founded by his uncle), legal adviser to the Congregation of Catholic Teaching and member of the Pontifical Commission for Social Communications. He is also a Privy Chamberlain of Sword and Cape and member of the College of Solicitors of the Sacred Consistory.

Glancing at the posts mentioned above, it is evident that Carlo Pacelli is present in nearly all the Vatican offices dealing with financial matters and in three of the most important ones. But while his position inside the Vatican is extremely strong, his participation in financial operations in Italy is limited if compared with that of his brothers and of the other Vatican lay financiers. He is president of the Compagnia di Roma Riassicurazioni (Roman re-insurance company) with a capital of 600 million lire,[1] and president of the publishing firm Gherardo Casini Editore (capital 50 million lire), and on the board of another big publishing firm, Sansoni. He also represents the Holy See on the board of directors of the Italian Home Ministry special fund for charity and religion in Rome.

Prince Marcantonio Pacelli has only one Vatican title, that of retired Brigadier General of the Noble Guard. But he is on the board of directors of the powerful building and real estate company Generale Immobiliare. The former president of Immobiliare, and now honorary president, Eugenio Gualdi, is on the board of directors of the Molini e Pastificio Pantanella, a flour and spaghetti producing company with a capital of 2 billion lire and of which Marcantonio Pacelli is president. Marcantonio Pacelli is also president of the Molini Antonio Biondi (capital 600 million lire), another big flour mill, and on the board of directors of Assicurazioni Generali (capital 14,520 million lire) and of Ceramica Pozzi (capital 22,841,040,000 lire) which make sanitary appliances. He is also on the board of IANA (Italo-Americana Nuovi Alberghi) which built the Hilton Hotel in Rome.

The third Pacelli brother, Giulio, also a lawyer, is legal representative to the administration of Propaganda Fide, a Colonel in the Noble Guard and Vatican representative to the International Institute for the Unification of Private Law.

In Italy he represents Vatican finances by sitting on the board of directors of one of Italy's largest banks, the Banco di Roma (capital 25 billion lire) and which is also tightly controlled by Vatican men. The Banco di Roma is presided over by lawyer Vittorino Veronese, a leading Catholic politician, former president of UNESCO, former president of Italian Catholic Action and adviser to the Vatican Secretariat for the Non-believers headed by the Austrian Cardinal Franziskus Koenig. The vice-president of the Banco di Roma is Massimo Spada, the top of the Vatican lay financiers. The Banco di Roma per la Svizzera, that is the Swiss branch of this Vatican-controlled bank, with a capital of 49 million

---

[1] In this chapter figures amounting to millions and billions of lire are given. For an easier understanding of their significance, it might be useful to mention that at the time the book went to press one billion lire was worth about £66,000 or $162,000, and a million lire about £6,600 or $16,200.

Swiss franks, has as its president Prince Giulio Pacelli and on the board of directors Massimo Spada and Luigi Mennini.

We find again Giulio Pacelli's name among the three vice-presidents of the Società Italiana per il Gas (capital 37,412 million lire) which is Italy's biggest domestic gas company, on whose board of directors there is Massimo Spada. Giulio Pacelli is also president of the Condil-Tubi, a company specializing in hydraulic works, with a capital of 250 million lire, and member of the executive committee of his brother Carlo's publishing firm Gherardo Casini Editore. He is president of the Istituo Farmacologico Serono, one of the biggest pharmaceutical companies in Italy, and on the board of Ferrovie del Sud-Est, an important railway company. He is vice-president of Cleda, a timber and tar company.

Having thus closed the chapter of nepotism in a literal sense, we proceed with nepotism in a wider sense. We have already mentioned the fact that one of the closest friends of Pope Pius was the Vatican architect Count Enrico Galeazzi on whom honours and jobs, mostly of a financial character, were bestowed. Let us now see how architect Galeazzi fares both inside and outside the Vatican.

To all practical purposes Enrico Galeazzi, as we have already noted, acted as Governor of the Vatican City State until the beginning of 1968. The post of Governor, traditionally held by an ecclesiastic, was left vacant by Pius XII in order to give Galeazzi a free hand with the title of Special Delegate. Count Galeazzi, as we said, is also the architect for the Sacred Apostolic Palaces, architect for the Fabbrica di San Pietro (that is for the structural upkeep of the basilica), member of the Pontifical Commission for the Protection of Historical and Artistic Monuments of the Holy See and member of the Pontifical Commission for Social Communications.

Galeazzi's position in the Italian financial world is in keeping with his Vatican status. He is very well placed in a few but very important key-posts of the big Italian concerns controlled by the Vatican. After he relinquished his post of Governor of the Vatican City, Count Galeazzi, aged seventy-three, was appointed president of Generale Immobiliare. Accordingly, while his position inside the Vatican was weakened, his control of Vatican investments was considerably strengthened. For Immobiliare, as it is known for short in Italy, is the main stronghold of the Vatican financial empire. The ties cannot be disputed. Not only was Galeazzi—who started out as one of the directors in 1944 and became vice-president in 1952—appointed president in 1968, but we find the company riddled with Vatican men. On the board of nine directors there are no less than four top Vatican financiers: Prince Marcantonio Pacelli, Signor Luigi Mennini (Special Delegate of the Institute for Religious Works), Marquis Giovanni Battista Sacchetti and Signor Luigi Quadrani. The latter is also secretary of the extraordinary section of the Administration of the Patrimony of the Apostolic See. Furthermore, at a lower level, in the College of Syndics of Immobiliare, we find Dr Guglielmo Mollari and Dr Francesco Falsini, who both work as accountants for the extraordinary section of the Vatican administration. To all practical purposes Immobiliare is a kind of subsidiary of the Vatican.

Immobiliare is one of the biggest and most successful real estate and building companies in the world. In 1969 this company was engaged in building hotels, blocks of flats for offices and private apartments, and in developing luxury residential areas all over Italy and particularly in Rome, Milan, Genoa, Turin, Florence, Naples, Palermo and Catania. The company, which has a capital of 67 billion lire, spent nearly 30 billion lire in 1967 for building projects in Italy.

Immobiliare owns the building firm SOGENE (capital 1 billion lire) which specializes in public works and which in 1967 carried out projects for 21.5 billion lire. It also owns the shares in a proportion that oscillates between 60 per cent to 100 per cent of the following companies:

1. Hotels

	Capital
IANA (Italo Americana Nuovi Alberghi)	2,000,000,000 (84.37%)
SIAM (Soc. Italiana Alberghi Moderni)	154,000,000 (99.45%)
Alberghi Ambrosiani, Milan	141,000,000 (99.93%)
Compagnia Italiana Alberghi Cavalieri	250,000,000 (99.86%)

2. Buildings

Urbanistica Sociale Torinese	1,200,000,000 (86.52%)
Immobiliare Pratolino, Florence	500,000,000 (90%)
R.C.S. (Restoration of Rome's Historical Centre)	100,000,000 (100%)

Immobiliare Fattoria di Carinate, Milan	200,000,000 (85%)
Comprensorio Tor Carbone, Rome	500,000,000 (60%)

3. *Industrial Companies*

SIAM (Metal furniture), Turin	503,000,000 (99.86%)
Bellrock Italiana (Cement partitions)	200,000,000 (100%)
Gessi San Salvo (Plaster)	112,000,000 (100%)

4. *Clinics*

Giuseppe Moscati, Rome	1,000,000,000 (92.08%)

Immobiliare also has an interest in many other companies of which we shall mention only the more important, giving in brackets Immobiliare's participation : Olgiata Romana, a very snobbish development plan around Rome's best golf course with a capital of 1½ billion lire (49.34 per cent); Società Edilizia Pineto, Rome, capital 1 billion lire (40 per cent); Sangone Po, Turin, capital 600 million (51 per cent); Ceramica Pozzi, sanitary appliances, capital 22 billion lire (22.15 per cent).

But the real turning point in the history of Immobiliare took place at the end of 1950 and the beginning of 1951 when the company decided to establish branches outside Italy. France was the first target, quickly followed by the USA and more recently Canada and Mexico. Contrary to gloomy predictions, according to which an Italian real estate and building company could not successfully compete against local firms, Immobiliare so far has done extremely well. Let us look at this success story country by country.

France

Immobiliare has established itself quite firmly in the very heart of Paris. The Company has already built, at 90 avenue des Champs Elysées, a huge block of flats for offices, shops and garages, part of which are rented to Pan American. It also bought adjoining properties at 61 rue de Ponthieu and 6 rue de Berry and they have been pulling down and rebuilding in this area a whole new block of offices and shops plus a cinema. A huge arcade links the three streets mentioned above.

The project has been carried out by Immobiliare-France, a

company that was formed in March 1967 with a capital of 11,400,000 francs. The money was not supplied directly from Rome, nor from the Vatican, but by the SGI (Società Generale Immobiliare) International Company, which is located, of all places, in Monrovia, Liberia, and which has a capital of $20 million. Immobiliare has also formed in Luxembourg the SGI International Holdings, which has a capital of $3 million and belongs entirely to the SGI International Company of Monrovia. The Luxembourg Company has the exclusive task of paying the interests and the amortization of a $20 million loan contracted by the Monrovia Company.

Canada

Immobiliare has built in Montreal the tallest skyscraper tower in the world (185 metres). It is located in the Place Victoria and it is called the Stock Exchange Tower because it houses both the Canadian and Montreal stock exchanges. The rest is formed by offices which Immobiliare leases. It belongs to the Place Victoria St Jacques Company, 95 per cent of which is owned by an Italian group led by Immobiliare (50.67 per cent) while the remaining 5 per cent is owned by the Rotterdamsche Bank. A twin skyscraper has been built in the same square.

Immobiliare also owns, through the Monrovia Company, the Redbrooke Estates Ltd (capital 6,833,000 Canadian dollars) which has built in Montreal the Port Royal Tower, and is selling its 224 apartments. Also in Montreal, SGI International owns 51.5 per cent of the Sogesan Constructions Ltd which is developing the Greensdale area by building a residential district.

USA

The bulk of Immobiliare's building activity is concentrated in Washington, mainly in the triangle formed by Virginia Avenue, New Hampshire Avenue and Rock Creek Parkway on the left bank of the Potomac. In this area Immobiliare has already built, is in the course of building or is planning to build, five huge blocks of flats for offices or private apartments. One of these blocks, The Watergate Hotel, numbers 240 flatlets and is run at a considerable profit by the company itself. Another block of flats for offices, already completed and entirely rented out, brings in an income of over $1 million a year.

Immobiliare has also started developing a residential area of 277 acres at Oyster Bay, near New York. The Oyster Bay Estate Inc., with a capital of $450,000, is entirely owned by SGI International.

Mexico

The most ambitious project in which Immobiliare is involved is that of Lomas Verdes, near Mexico City, where a satellite city of 100,000 inhabitants is being built. To this end, a company has been formed, the Lomas Verdes SAICV (capital 100,999,600 pesos), in which SGI International has a participation of 28.19 per cent, while a group of other Italian companies has 16.69 per cent and local investors the remaining 55.12 per cent. They include Signor Pagliari, the husband of Merle Oberon.

Returning to our Vatican lay financiers : Count Galeazzi is also on the board of the already mentioned SOGENE, of which Eugenio Gualdi is president and in which Marcantonio Pacelli is also on the board, he is on the board of INVEST (capital 20,200 million lire), a real estate investment company, and on the board of another national Italian bank, the Credito Italiano, with a capital of 30 billion lire. The Italian branch of the Radio Corporation of America (RCA Italiana) has as its president the Vatican architect Enrico Galeazzi, reportedly on the suggestion of his old and close friend, the late Cardinal Spellman.[2] Galeazzi is on the board of CIT, the Italian National Tourist Office, of Acqua Pia supplying water to the city of Rome, of the big insurance company Riunione Adriatica di Sicurtà (Massimo Spada was the former president), of the Romana Finanziaria SIFIR, and of the Olgiata Romana.

We have been dealing so far with a group of four Vatican financiers, the three Pacelli plus Count Galeazzi, who have been very much in the public eye both because of the posts they hold in the Vatican and because they were protégés of Pius XII. But this is far from being the end of the story. A much better picture of the extent of Vatican penetration into Italian economy can be formed through the meteoric rise to dizzy financial heights of two former humble employees of the Vatican Bank and of the Institute for Religious Works. According to the Pontifical Yearbook of 1945,

[2] Or possibly through the powerful and very wealthy Order of the Knights of Columbus, which Galeazzi represents at the Holy See.

the Institute had as its second accountant Signor Massimo Spada, while one of the book-keepers was Signor Giulio Mennini. There was no other mention of them as holders of other Vatican jobs or titles, nor did they appear on any of the boards of directors of Italian companies.

Let us look at their position twenty-five years later, starting with Massimo Spada.

Before Pius XII founded the Institute for Religious Works in 1942, the Vatican used to carry out its business through a few trusted Roman stockbrokers, among whom was Luigi Spada, Massimo's father. When the Institute was set up, the stockbroker's son was given a minor clerical job. Today Massimo Spada is no longer with the Institute but occupies several important posts in the Vatican financial organization.

Massimo Spada is administrative adviser to the Pontifical Society for the Preservation of the Faith and for the Building of New Churches in Rome, member of the administrative council of the Rome diocese and represents the Holy See on the board of directors of the special fund of the Italian Home Office for charity and religion in Rome. He was appointed Privy Chamberlain of Sword and Cape, one of the highest Vatican titles, in 1963, a title which his brother Filippo also holds.

All this, you might say, is fairly natural. It is natural that a minor employee, if he has a talent for administration, should achieve a good position after twenty-four years of service. This is true. But what interests us more—and what gives us a strong clue as to how and where Vatican money is invested in Italy—is the truly impressive range of positions Massimo Spada today occupies in the Italian financial and industrial world.

To begin with, it seems rather obvious that a bank called Banca Cattolica del Veneto (capital 3 billion lire) should have as its president the Vatican financier Massimo Spada. It is also obvious that the publishing firm Impianti Tipografici Lombardi (capital 300 million lire), whose president is Mgr Luigi Oldani and whose vice-president is Mgr Giuseppe Bicchierai, should have Massimo Spada on the board of directors.

Less to be expected is the fact that one of the biggest Italian insurance companies, the Riunione Adriatica di Sicurtà (capital 4,320 million lire), should have had, until three years ago, as its president and managing director, Massimo Spada. Still in the insurance field, we find Spada to be president and managing director of L'Assicuratrice Italiana (capital 1,200 million lire), vice-president of Lavoro e Sicurtà (capital 750 million lire), vice-president of the Unione Subalpina di Assicurazioni (capital 480 million lire) and on the boards of directors of the Unione Italiana di Riassicurazione (capital 600 million lire) and of L'Italica Assicurazioni (capital 100 million lire).[3]

In the banking field, the hold the Vatican has on Banco di Roma through the president Vittorino Veronese and Prince Giulio Pacelli is further strengthened, as we saw, by the presence of Spada as vice-president. Massimo Spada is also vice-president of the Istituto Bancario Italiano (capital 10 billion lire), and of the Credito Commerciale di Cremona (capital 2 billion lire), and he is on the board of directors of the Banca Privata Finanziaria (capital 1 billion lire).

Vatican capital is also represented, through Massimo Spada, in the financing business. He appears as a member of the board of directors of the powerful financial holding Società Meridionale Finanziaria, which has a capital of 122 billion lire, and of the Instituto Centrale Finanziario (capital 150 million lire), and as vice-president of the Finanziaria Industriale e Commerciale.

Vatican capital could not fail to be present in the petroleum industry and we thus find that Massimo Spada is on the board of directors of Shell Italiana, the Italian subsidiary of the Royal Dutch Shell Company, with a capital of 129 billion lire invested in Italy.

The presence of Spada on the board of directors of the Società Italiana per il Gas (capital 37,412 million lire) and on which Prince Giulio Pacelli is vice-president, confirms the Vatican financial involvement in this firm.

In order to prove that the Catholic Church has, in the matter of investments, very catholic tastes, we shall mention that Massimo Spada is the president of the big car factory Lancia (capital 10,800 million lire), president of the Vianini (capital 5 billion lire) building firm, on the boards of Tosi Franco (capital 2,500 million) which specializes in steel foundries, boilers and timber, of the cotton

[3] The posts held by Spada and other characters have been checked in the 1968 edition of *Guida Monaci*, Italy's foremost reference book. Whenever possible they have been brought up to date.

mills Vittorio Olcese (capital 5 billion lire), of the Siemens Elettra (capital 4 billion lire) and of the Bocciardo Sebastiano company that deals with skins and leather.

Massimo Spada, who evidently must have inherited from St Anthony of Padua the gift of ubiquity, is president of the Capitolina Finanziaria (a Roman financing firm), of the Salifera Siciliana (which produces salt in Sicily), vice-president of the Banca Provinciale Lombarda, managing director of the Assicuratrice Italiana, administrator of the telegraph company Italcable, and of Italmobiliare (a financial holding with 15 billion lire capital), and is on the boards of Italcementi, Fabbriche Riunite Cemento, Società Italiana Strade Ferrate Meridionali (a South Italian railway company), of Mediobanca (banking), of FIDIA (an investment company), of the powerful SNIA-Viscosa (artificial textiles and plastics), of the Compagnia Generale Dolciaria (sweets) and of ITALPI (industrial shares). He also finds time to be on the board of directors of the well-known Milan clinic La Madonnina.

Probably the only concern that Signor Spada runs as president without Vatican support is the Progredi, a firm with a capital of only 48 million lire and which acts as consultant in technical, organizational and management problems, a profession to which, in view of his brilliant achievements, he seems to be very much entitled.

I have deliberately saved as the final big bang in Massimo Spada's financial fireworks the fact that he is on the board of directors of FINSIDER, a State-controlled company with 195 billion lire capital. FINSIDER is part of IRI, the Istituto per la Ricostruzione Industriale (Institute for Industrial Reconstruction), which was formed during the Fascist regime to save Italian industries on the verge of bankruptcy and to stimulate industrial production as a whole.

After the war Italy's democratic Governments found IRI to be a very useful tool and not only kept it alive but increased its range of action. IRI today controls, among innumerable other things, the biggest Italian shipyards, the shipping line Italia, the air company Alitalia, Alfa Romeo, the Autostrada del Sole and other autostrade and the entire telephone system. It is the biggest Italian cartel, with Fiat coming second. IRI is a strange combination of Government control and planning and of private capital and initiative. For every lira produced by the State, IRI has been able to borrow another

12 lire from the banks, the big financiers and from small private investors. The IRI bonds give a tax-free dividend of 5 to 6 per cent, and the Vatican owns quite a number.

The backbone of IRI is FINSIDER, which produces over 90 per cent of Italy's steel. Although Italy has no natural resources of coal or iron ore worth mentioning, FINSIDER has managed to produce steel at competitive international prices. It imports coal and iron ore from abroad by sea, the cheapest form of transport. On the shore, four giant smelting works stand ready to receive the raw materials.[4] Not only does FINSIDER supply almost the entire internal market, but it produces a surplus for export. Naturally, there are other Italian steelworks, mostly dealing with scrap iron, that make up for the gap in internal consumption and allow FINSIDER to export.

But all this is largely irrelevant. What matters is that IRI, besides being the biggest Italian industrial concern, is also the biggest financial holding and that it either entirely owns or controls, by holding the majority of the bonds or shares, a very large number of Italian companies or financial institutions. And what matters even more is that Vatican capital, represented by Massimo Spada on the board of directors of FINSIDER, is present in this field as well.

I shall quote as a typical example the case of the Banco di Santo Spirito. It has a capital of 8 billion lire and, despite its appealing name, it does not perform miracles, nor does it give you an interest higher than that of any other bank. It was founded in 1605.

Quite recently, when it was mentioned in the press that the Banco di Santo Spirito was controlled by the Vatican, a Catholic newsagency denied it, pointing out that 99.96 per cent of the bank's capital belonged to IRI. Correct. But it did not mention that IRI has on the board of directors of its main holding, FINSIDER, Signor Massimo Spada and that the bank itself has as its president Marquis Giovanni Battista Sacchetti and on its board of directors Signor Luigi Mennini, both of them top Vatican personalities. Another link between IRI and the Vatican can be found in the fact that Vittorino Veronese, President of the Banco di Roma, and Professor Silvio Golzio, President of the Credito Italiano, two major IRI banks, are members of the wealthy Pius XII Foundation for the Apostolate of Laymen. It was founded in 1953 by Pope Pius who

---

[4] At Cornigliano, Piambino, Bagnoli and Taranto.

endowed it with a considerable initial capital, later swelled by legacies and donations. Until 1969 the President of the Foundation was Massimo Spada with Carlo Pacelli on the board. Now they are both out, and the presidency has been taken over by Cardinal Villot.

The career of Luigi Mennini, although on a smaller scale, runs parallel to that of Massimo Spada. In 1943 he was a mere book-keeper in the Institute for Religious Works. Today we find that he has become delegate of the Institute, which in Vatican jargon means *deus ex machina*, he was made a Privy Chamberlain of Sword and Cape on 22 June 1963 (the same day as Spada and Vittorino Veronese) and he acts as consultant to the administrative section of the Congregation of the Clergy which, as we saw, carries out important financial functions. He is also president of the Peregrinatio Romana ad Petri Sedem, an organization which finances pilgrimages to Rome.

In Italy Signor Mennini, besides being, as we have seen, on the board of directors of such Vatican strongholds as the Immobiliare, the Swiss branch of Banco di Roma and the Banco di Santo Spirito, holds several posts in other financial organizations. He is vice-president of the Instituto Centrale Finanziario (capital 150 million lire)[5] with Spada on the board; he is on the board of directors of the Finanziaria Industriale e Commerciale (capital 300 million); and also on the board, with the ubiquitous Massimo Spada, of CIM, a big chain of stores and supermarkets (capital 750 million lire), and the sole administrator of SGIR Società Gestione Immobili Roma, a small company with a capital of only 7 million lire, but which has the important task of administering Vatican real estate in Rome. Mennini appears on the board of EFIBANCA (a kind of banking pool), he is the syndic of Compagnia San Giorgio (capital 100 million), which has as managing director Mgr Giorgio Roche, and syndic of Cementerie Siciliane of the Pesenti group.

When dealing with the Banco di Santo Spirito we mentioned that its president is Marquis Giovanni Battista Sacchetti and we have thus brought into the story another of the leading Vatican financiers. The marquis used to hold the post of Foriere Maggiore of the Sacred Apostolic Palaces, which was recently abolished. In the old

[5] Also on the board of directors there is Antonio Rinaldi, administrative councillor of the Congregation for the Clergy and co-director general of Banco di Roma.

days the Foriere Maggiore was in charge of the structural upkeep of the Apostolic Palaces, besides water supply and the furniture of the same. He belonged to the exclusive 'club' of the Privy Chamberlains of Sword and Cape Participating (eight all told) who used to wear a special costume and had a place of honour during official papal functions. Pope Paul has changed the medieval title into the more prosaic one of 'Gentlemen of His Holiness', and has abolished the costume. He is also a member of the Heraldic Commission of the Pontifical Court which has, among other things, the task of advising on the design of the coats of arms of new Pontiffs and Cardinals.

Much more substantial is Sacchetti's presence in the Italian financial world. Besides being president of the Banco di Santo Spirito and on the board of directors of Immobiliare, he is also president of the Condotte d'Acque (capital 7 billion lire), a big building and public works firm which made the Mont Blanc road tunnel on the Italian side, president of the Mediocredito Regionale del Lazio, a company that finances medium and small industries in the region of Latium, and president of Laziale Beni Immobili (real estate), also president of the Roman section of UCID Unione Cristiana Imprenditori e Dirigenti (Christian Union of Business-men and Executives) and president of the Opera Pia degli Infermi di S Giovanni dei Fiorentini, a Catholic hospitalization agency. Marquis Sacchetti, like Massimo Spada, Vittorino Veronese and Prince Carlo Pacelli, represents the Holy See on the board of directors of the Italian Home Ministry special fund for charity and the promotion of religion in the city of Rome.

I have been endeavouring, up to this point, to illustrate the connections that exist between two worlds : that of the Vatican financial organization and that of the Italian banking, financial, insurance and business enterprises. In order to do so I have chosen just a few of the most representative and important characters who most ostensibly represent this link.

In doing so I might have missed several minor and perhaps even a few major connections. But, all told, I think I have given the reader a fair idea of how deeply and substantially the men con-nected with Vatican finances are involved in Italian business life. There are, of course, many more, as there are indirect and subtle links between Vatican capital and Italian business which are more difficult to pin down but which nevertheless exist.

One of these links, not so much subtle as very powerful, is represented by Carlo Pesenti. He is the king of Italy's cement industry and one of the richest men in the country. He well deserves to be on the executive committee of the Confindustria, Italy's association of industrialists. Pesenti is president of Italcementi, the firm around which his financial empire revolves and which has a nominal capital of 32 billion lire. Pesenti keeps a very tight hold on it by his position of managing director with nobody else on the board, and also director-general. The same applies to the Italian Portland Cement (capital 300 million lire) which Pesenti runs single-handed.

Pesenti has his fingers in many other concerns and particularly those in which Vatican capital is invested. In the Credito Commerciale di Cremona (capital 2 billion lire) of which, as we saw, Spada is the vice-president, Pesenti appears on the board of directors. Both Pesenti and Spada are on the board of Tosi Franco (capital 2,500 million), the big boiler-making firm. And to confirm, if it were necessary, Pesenti's involvement with Vatican capital, we shall mention that he is also on the board of directors of the key Vatican-controlled company, Immobiliare.

Carlo Pesenti is also vice-president of the Riunione Adriatica di Sicurtà (of which Spada was president), on the board of EFIBANCA (with Mennini), of Strade Ferrate Meridionali (with Spada), of ITALPI (with Spada), of Compagnia Generale Dolciaria (with Spada) and of Banca Provinciale Lombarda (Spada being vice-president).

The Pesenti group during the last few years has acquired control of several other banks besides the ones mentioned above. At the end of 1967 he has merged into one the following banks : Credito di Venezia e Rio della Plata, Venice (3,200 million lire); Banca Romana, Rome (1,500 million); Istituto Bancario Romano, Rome (500 million); Credito Mobiliare Fiorentino, Florence (700 million); Banca Torinese Balbis e Guglielmone, Turin (1,500 million); Banca di Credito e Risparmio, Rome (1,500 million); Banca di Credito Genovese, Genoa (700 million); Banca Naef-Ferrazzi-Longhi, La Spezia (400 million). Thus the group, in which the Vatican is strongly represented, has become the owner of one of the biggest private banks in Italy, capable of competing with the national banks controlled by the State.

The new bank, called Istituto Bancario Italiano, is presided over by Carlo Pesenti, with Massimo Spada as one of the two vice-presidents and Marquis Travaglini di Santa Rita on the board of directors. It has a capital of 10 billion lire controlled by the financial holding Italmobiliare (Pesenti is president and Spada is on the board) which in turn belongs to Italcementi. Italmobiliare also owns a chain of restaurants including Milan's famous Biffi. Pesenti used to own the automobile company Lancia, of which Spada was president, but in 1969, as the company was losing money, he sold it to Fiat.

Other posts held by Pesenti are: president of Natro Cellulosa Industria Imballaggi Carta (capital 1,200 million lire), which makes the sacks for the cement; president of Imballaggi Carta, and Industria Meridionale Imballaggi, both making paper sacks; managing director and general director of CASA (capital 960 million lire), a cement-making firm; president of Officine Trasformatori Elettrici, electric transformers (capital 300 million lire); sole managing director of CIDI, quick-lime production (capital 90 million lire), and a member of the board of directors of the big Falk steel foundries. He is vice-president of Società Autoferriere Bergamo (transport); Cementerie delle Puglie, Cementerie Apuane and of Sacelit (cement). He is on the board of Industrie Tessili Italiane (textiles); the Credito Commerciale (banking); the Cartiere Burgo (paper mill) and ITALPI—Officine Elettriche Genovesi (electric equipment).

None of the top Vatican financiers appears on the boards of the companies listed above and it is therefore uncertain whether Vatican capital is invested in them, through Pesenti, or not.

To continue this game of tracing connections between the world of the Vatican and that of Italian finance, I shall mention two companies which are controlled by members of the Black Aristocracy. One is the Cassa di Risparmio di Roma (Rome Savings Bank) which was founded in 1936 under Pope Gregory XVI and which, besides functioning as a bank, runs nine pawnshops in the city of Rome and four more in the province—the so-called 'Monti di Pietà'. The bank was presided over by Marquis Giuseppe della Chiesa, who died in 1966 and whose family was made illustrious by Pope Benedict XV (1914–22). Among the members of the board of directors there is Prince Urbano Barberini (Pope Urban VIII was a Barberini) who is president of the Pontificia Insigne Accademia dei Virtuosi al Pantheon, Count Stanislao Pecci (Leo XIII was a Pecci) who is Special Envoy and Minister Plenipotentiary of the Knights of Malta to the Holy See, Count Luigi Macchi di Cellere, Balì of the Knights of Malta, and Marquis Francesco Maria Theodoli, member of the Heraldic Commission of the Pontifical Court and honorary retired colonel of the Noble Guard.

The late Marquis della Chiesa was also president of the Istituto Romano di Beni Stabili, a powerful real estate company with a capital of 24 billion lire. On the board of directors of this company we find Count Francesco Cantuti di Castelvetri, the commander (with the rank of colonel) of the Palatine Guard, and two more members of the Black Aristocracy, namely Marquis Giacinto Guglielmi and Prince Ludovico Spada Veralli Potenziani.

The position that Marquis della Chiesa held in the Italian financial world was almost as strong as that of Massimo Spada, although his ties with the Vatican were slighter. He was president of the Istituto di Credito delle Casse di Risparmio Italiane (capital 17,940 million lire) which finances Italian savings banks; president of the Federazione delle Casse di Risparmio dell'Italia Centrale, that is, the federation of the savings banks of Central Italy; president of Praevidentia (capital 250 million), another savings bank; and president of the Istituto Federale di Credito Agrario per l'Italia Centrale (on whose board there is Count Stanislao Pecci) which advances money to farmers in Central Italy. In the building field, Marquis della Chiesa was president of Cogeco (capital 500 million lire) and of ICLA (capital 200 million lire).

The Marquis was also vice-president of SARA (capital 1½ billion lire), a road-building firm which is currently making the Rome–Aquila autostrada; on the board of the Istituto Nazionale Credito per il Lavoro Italiano all'Estero (capital 774 million lire) which finances Italian firms working abroad; on the board of the Consorzio Nazionale per il Credito Agrario di Miglioramento (capital 13 billion lire) which finances land reclamation; and on the board of Fiduciaria Mobiliare e Immobiliare (capital 100 million lire), a credit and real estate company. His standing was so high that the Italian Government appointed him to the National Council for Economy and Labour, a very important consultative body.

We must now be cautious. The presence of Vatican lay financiers as chairmen, vice-chairmen or on the board of directors of the companies mentioned above does not necessarily mean that Vatican capital is actually invested in every one of the said companies. In some cases it may have happened that the Vatican lay financiers, having first occupied strong and sometimes key positions in Italian companies thanks to the Vatican capital they represented, have then branched off in other directions on their own initiative. In other cases, Italian companies which have little to do with Vatican capital have invited Vatican men to become directors for prestige reasons.

But the picture we have drawn so far, even if incomplete, gives us an idea of the extent of Vatican financial involvement in Italy, of the spheres of economy preferred and of the channels chosen to operate. In order to recapitulate and to move on to safe ground, we shall list below the main fields of activity in which the Vatican operates and the firms on which it exercises a tighter control.

Banking	Banco di Santo Spirito Banco di Roma Istituto Bancario Italiano Banca Cattolica del Veneto Cassa di Risparmio di Roma
Insurance	Riunione Adriatica di Sicurtà Assicurazioni Generali L'Assicuratrice Italiana Compagnia di Roma Riassicurazioni
Financing	SME Istituto Centrale Finanziario Finanziaria Industriale e Commerciale INVEST
Steel industry	FINSIDER (IRI)
Real estate	Immobiliare Istituto Romano di Beni Stabili Società Gestione Immobili Roma
Cement	The Pesenti group

Building	SOGENE Condotte d'Acqua Vianini
Flour and spaghetti	Molini e Pastificio Pantanella Molini Antonio Biondi
Gas	Società Italiana per il Gas
Textiles	Vittorio Olcese
Mechanical industry	Tosi Franco

Before the recent nationalizations, Vatican capital was also conspicuously present in the electrical and telephone companies. More capital was invested in private companies supplying water, gas, domestic electricity and public transport to Rome and other Italian cities, but most of these services have since been taken over by the municipalities.

The overall criterion has been that of playing it safe. People, the Vatican financiers appear to have reasoned, will always eat bread and spaghetti, use gas, water and electricity, make telephone calls, take buses and trams, buy or rent apartments, shops and offices, go to hotels (the Vatican, through Immobiliare, has an interest in the Hilton hotel in Rome[6] and in the CIGA—Compagnia Italiana Grandi Alberghi—which controls some of the best hotels in Italy), buy clothes, open bank accounts, invest in insurance policies, use sanitary appliances (Ceramica Pozzi) and, if pushed, pawn their wristwatches, cameras or jewels. This last remark is perhaps unfair, as the main object of the pawn shops is to protect poor people from private moneylenders. Nevertheless they charge 8 per cent interest plus expenses.

The idea is to invest money in companies that cater for basic human needs, companies that do not follow fashions, that therefore will not bring in sensational dividends but are fundamentally sound. It is a long-range, cautious and possibly over-cautious policy, but an understandable one and perhaps inevitable. The ecclesiastics in charge of the Administration of the Holy See Property, of the Special Administration and of the Vatican bank are, after all,

[6] Built by Italo-Americani Nuovi Alberghi, of which Eugenio Gualdi is president and which has Marcantonio Pacelli on the board.

handling funds that are not their own. They have the mentality of a trustee, rather than that of a gambler.

To complete the picture one must note that, since the end of the war, Vatican financiers have found themselves in an exceptionally privileged position. The Christian Democrats, Italy's strongest party, have been uninterruptedly in office since 1945, either alone or as leaders of a Centre or Centre-Left coalition. This means that a series of Catholic Prime Ministers, of Ministers of Finances, Treasury, Public Works, Industry and Commerce, Foreign Trade, etc., their Under Secretaries and top civil servants have been for the last decades staunch Catholics ready to view the financial activities of the Holy See with a more than sympathetic eye. The same can be said of the regional authorities and of the executives of the *enti parastatali*, the State-controlled agencies.

The system worked, and still works, both ways. The support of the Catholic Church at various levels, from the Vatican itself down to the parish priests, can be equally useful in enabling an ambitious politician to get a ministry, if not even the premiership, or to be elected to parliament, as for a humble citizen to get a job or a pension. A typical joke current in Italian business circles goes as follows : two Milanese businessmen meet on the sleeping car going from Rome to Milan. One of them is dejected and furious.

'This damned city should be razed to the ground. I spent two weeks in Rome, I was sent from one office to another, I wasted hours waiting for Government officials who didn't turn up. I've been going round and round in circles without getting anywhere. And how did it go with you?'

'Oh,' said the other, all smiles, 'I arrived in Rome this morning and, as you see, I'm going back tonight after having settled all I came here to do.'

'But that's fantastic! How did you manage it?'

'Well, it's simple. When I go to Rome I always hire a car to meet me at the station. . . .'

'So do I, of course.'

'Then I hire a secretary to take short-hand notes.'

'So do I, but it doesn't help.'

'Aha, but, you see, I also hire a priest.'

The image of the priest as a person steeped in worldly affairs, connected with politics and business, as a busy-body and an intermediary freely mixing the sacred and the profane, is only too frequent in Rome. It has lent itself to another joke. When the Romans see the big shiny black cars allotted to Cardinals and other top Vatican officials go by, they say that the initials on the plate, scv (Stato Città del Vaticano), mean : 'Se Cristo vedesse!' ('If Christ could only see this!').

In all fairness it must be said that while the Vatican has no doubt taken advantage of the privileged position in which it has found itself, it has done so in a correct way. No Vatican lay financier has ever been embroiled in any of the big scandals that have been plagueing post-war, democratic Italy. We shall mention just a few of the more outstanding ones : the scandal connected with the building of the Fiumicino international airport; the tobacco monopoly; the banana monopoly; the one involving the Nuclear Energy Commission; the Health Institute; the scandal of the tubercular children 'sold' by a doctor in the social insurance service (Previdenza Sociale) to phoney clinics that made an incredible profit out of them; the collapse of the Vajont dyke in which three thousand people were killed, and the big scandal of the Bank of Sicily.

Marquis Giovanni Battista Sacchetti, president of the Banco di Santo Spirito, was one of the thirty-eight defendants at the Bank of Sicily trial, charged with embezzlement of public funds. He emerged unblemished at the end of the trial in 1969 with a full acquittal.

The only big issue which has so far raised considerable doubts about its correctness was the exemption granted by the Italian Government to the Vatican from paying taxes on the dividends of shares the Vatican holds in Italy. It was all arranged in a rather underhand way and we shall deal with it in the next chapter as it will give us the opportunity of assessing, if only in part, the amount of capital invested by the Vatican in Italy.

9

Do Not Give Unto Caesar

Napoleon, before meeting his doom at Waterloo, reinstated the Pope in his domains. Mussolini, shortly before he was overthrown by the Fascist Grand Council and arrested by the carabinieri of King Victor Emmanuel III, did something similar, although on a much smaller scale. He exempted the Holy See from paying taxes on the dividends of shares owned in Italy. He had probably already realized that the war against the Allies was lost and wanted to keep well in with Pius XII in view of a possible peace treaty negotiated through the Vatican.

A special tax on dividends had been imposed by the Fascist Government in September 1935. The companies paying out had to deduct, first 10 per cent, later 20 per cent, at source and give this to the Finance Ministry. It was called *cedolare* because it was applied when the investors cashed the coupons (*cedole*) of their shares. The Vatican, which at the time was still somewhat awed by the Fascist regime, raised no objection and allowed the tax to be regularly collected.

On a circular dated 31 December 1942, referring to a law dated 2 October 1942, the Finance Ministry instructed all competent offices to exempt the Holy See from paying the *cedolare*. The circular was signed by the then director general of the Finance Ministry who was called, quite appropriately, Buoncristiano (Goodchristian). The circular also specified which were the organizations that came under the heading of Holy See. It listed the Holy Office, the Consistorial Congregation, the Congregation of the Council, the Congregation of the Religious, Propaganda Fide, the Congregation for the Seminaries and Universities of Studies and the Congregation for the upkeep of St Peter's. It added the Vatican tribunals Apostolic Penitentiary, Apostolic Signature and the Sacra Rota and the following offices: Apostolic Chancery, Apostolic

119

Datary, the Reverend Apostolic Chamber, the Secretariat of State, the Administration of the Holy See Properties, the Special Administration and the Institute for Religious Works. After this last item was a parenthesis '(inasmuch as it administers funds belonging to the Holy See)'. The words in parentheses are rather interesting as they show that the Fascist Government intended to make a distinction between the financial operations and investments carried out by the Vatican bank on behalf of the Holy See and those carried out on behalf of its other clients.

We have been dealing with this little known and apparently outdated document because it is the starting point and the basis of a much more recent and publicized *imbroglio* which has involved the Vatican on one side and several top Italian politicians on the other and has induced beatniks and hippies to wear a badge saying TAX THE VATICAN.

On 29 December 1962 the Italian Government again taxed dividends, claiming first 15 per cent, later increasing this to 30 per cent. The 30 per cent tax favoured the big industrialists because it exempted them from declaring their dividends in their income tax returns. And as income tax is cumulative, most of the industrialists would have had to pay much more than 30 per cent. This was done to stimulate investments at a time when Italian economy was going through a depression, and it has, with other financial measures, achieved that aim. Italy's economy has, since 1965, started expanding again at the rate of over 5 per cent a year. But for the Vatican, which didn't pay income tax, it represented a net loss of 30 per cent.

The Vatican again accepted the imposition of the *cedolare* without protesting, at least officially. But then it embarked on negotiations with the Italian Government which were conducted with the usual ability and discretion. They were concluded in October 1963 with an exchange of notes between the then Secretary of State Cardinal Cicognani and the Italian Ambassador to the Holy See, Bartolomeo Migone. Here is the text of Cicognani's note, pruned of a few technical details. (The translations which follow reflect the stilted and involved style of the originals.)

From the Vatican
11 October 1963

Signor Ambassador,

With the law of 2 October 1942, issued in the spirit of the Concordat, the coupons of the shares belonging to the Holy See were exempted from paying taxes. The recent law of 29 December 1962, which introduced a tax on the dividends distributed by companies, is now attracting in its field of application also the dividends pertaining to the Holy See.

In the spirit of our Concordat and considering the law of 2 October 1942, it would be desirable that a favourable treatment be granted to the Holy See.

I, therefore, suggest : that the aforementioned tax on dividends shall not be applied, starting from the date it was instituted, to the profits distributed under any form by the companies and pertaining to the Holy See. And that one shall consider as included in the denomination 'Holy See' the Supreme Pontiff, the Sacred Congregations, the Tribunals and the central offices specified in the circular of 31 December 1942, through which the Supreme Pontiff governs the Catholic Church and looks after the affairs of the same.

If the Italian Government should accept the proposal contained in the present letter, I would beg you to give kind confirmation.

Please accept, Signor Ambassador, the expression of my highest consideration.

A. G. Cardinal Cicognani

The same day the Italian Ambassador replied :

Rome
11 October 1963

Your Very Reverend Eminence,

I have the honour to inform you that I have received your letter of today and which runs as follows : (here comes the full text of Cicognani's letter in inverted commas).

I have the honour to inform Your Very Reverend Eminence that the Italian Government is agreed on what forms the object of the aforementioned note.

Please accept, Very Reverend Eminence, the expressions of my highest consideration and devout homage.

Migone

At the time Italy was ruled by a minority, a stop-gap, all-Christian Democrat Government headed by Giovanni Leone and which, because of its very nature, was not supposed to take on such heavy commitments. The whole thing was kept secret. Neither Parliament nor public opinion were informed. About a year later, on 13 November 1963, the Finance Minister Mario Martinelli sent a circular to the Association of Registered Companies and to the Association of Banks instructing them not to deduct 30 per cent from the dividends of shares belonging to the Holy See. It is a document (I have a photostat) which is quite incredible on two counts : firstly, the exchange of notes between Cardinal Cicognani and Ambassador Migone had not been approved by Parliament, which knew nothing about it, and had therefore no juridical value. Secondly, the Government had resigned *eight days before* Martinelli signed the circular ! In a way he was no longer Finance Minister and should have limited himself to a strictly routine administration instead of creating a *fait accompli* on an issue of such importance.

When Christian Democrat Aldo Moro formed a Centre-Left coalition with the Christian Democrats, the Saragat Socialists, the Nenni Socialists and the Republicans, a new Finance Minister, Roberto Tremelloni (a Saragat Socialist), took the place of Martinelli. Tremelloni discovered the existence of the Martinelli circular and was horrified. He threatened to resign if the circular was not immediately withdrawn. Moro succeeded in soothing him and tried to find a compromise solution, an activity in which he excels. For months discussions and negotiations went on behind the scenes among Moro, Tremelloni, Saragat, Nenni and the Vatican.

The solution suggested by Moro was the following : the Italian Government would present to Parliament a law to ratify the exchange of notes and thus make the Martinelli circular legal, even if only retrospectively; the Vatican should inform the Government of the exact amount of shares owned so that, at least, the Government should know and be able to tell Parliament what it was exempting. The compromise was rejected both by Cardinal Cicognani, who refused to reveal the full extent of Vatican investments, and by the Socialists in the Government. The Budget Minister Antonio Giolitti and his Under-Secretary Luigi Anderlini, both Nenni Socialists, were strongly opposed.

In June 1964 the Government was overthrown and Moro formed

a second Centre-Left coalition from which the left wing of the Nenni Socialists was excluded. Giolitti was substituted by Giovanni Pieraccini, who was a little less adamant. And then, according to what the former Budget Under Secretary Luigi Anderlini told me, the Vatican threatened, if it did not get its way, to throw on the market all the shares it possessed. The stock market was going through a severe crisis and the shares had dropped on average by about 40 per cent. Had the Vatican threat been carried out it could have had disastrous consequences for Italian economy.

The Italian Government was forced to surrender, not unwillingly on the part of the Christian Democrats. On 26 October 1964 a law draft was prepared to ratify the exchange of diplomatic notes between Cardinal Cicognani and Ambassador Migone. The draft was signed by Socialist Giuseppe Saragat as Foreign Minister and by Roberto Tremelloni, also a Socialist, as Finance Minister and was approved by the Cabinet. But that is as far as it went. The law draft remained a draft because it was never submitted to Parliament, which could have approved it, rejected or modified it. Meanwhile the Vatican continued enjoying the tax exemption.

It was only in January 1968 that another transition, all-Christian Democrat Government, led again by Giovanni Leone, put an end to the exemption. The Prime Minister disposed of the whole controversial issue with one short sentence. In introducing to Parliament the programme of his Government, Leone said : 'The Government will not present the law draft to ratify the exchange of notes and therefore the Holy See will pay the tax as established by law.' The Vatican reaction, considering both the amount of money and the question of principle involved, was rather mild. There was no official diplomatic protest or, if there was, it was not made public. The Vatican spokesman Mgr Vallainc said that the exemption was justified both by the letter and the spirit of the Concordat and by the fact that the Holy See should be considered as a welfare agency. He added that the Italian State should have taken into consideration the considerable amount of foreign currency brought to Italy by pilgrims and tourists coming to Rome to see the Pope and the Vatican and the fact that the Vatican, by investing its capital in Italy, was stimulating the economic development of the country. Anyhow, while upholding in principle the right to be exempted, the Vatican did not refuse to pay the tax on dividends and merely asked the Finance Ministry to be allowed to pay the arrears in easy instalments, a request which I understand was granted.

But, leaving aside these rather dubious dealings, for which the Italian Government rather than the Vatican is to blame, how much did the exemption amount to? On 16 March 1967, the Finance Minister Luigi Preti, answering a question in the Senate, gave the following figures:

Administration of the Holy See Patrimony:	340,000
Institute for Religious Works:	1,849,360,971
Propaganda Fide:	21,810,035
Fabbrica di San Pietro:	1,323,851
Special Administration:	1,389,448,564
Pontifical Society for St Peter Apostle:	44,000
Total lire:	3,262,327,421

These figures are extremely interesting as they provide us with some sort of key to the extent of Vatican investments in Italy. First of all it must be noted that the 3,262 million refers to three preceding years and that the figure must be divided by three to get an approximate yearly average. It works out at 1,087 million. But as the figures refer to only 30 per cent of the dividends, one must multiply it by 3.3 to get an idea of the value of the dividends the Vatican reaps in Italy every year. It works out at 3,581 million lire. As the Italian shares bring in on average a dividend of about 4 per cent, the value of the Vatican investment in shares can be assessed approximately at 89,525 million lire.

The correctness of this calculation was confirmed nearly a year later, that is on 23 February 1968, by the same Finance Minister Preti, who, taking part in a debate of the Parliamentary Committee for Foreign Affairs, said that the Holy See owned shares worth approximately 100 billion lire and which brought in a dividend of 3 to 4 billion a year. Large as it is, this sum does not come anywhere near representing the real wealth of the Vatican.

In the first place the figures mentioned do not necessarily correspond to the whole amount invested by Vatican financiers in Italian private shares. By Italian Stock Exchange regulations, one is allowed not to collect the dividends for five years and an extension to six or seven years can be easily obtained. To avoid cashing in the dividends every year is a fairly common practice. Suppose that a building contractor has made a great deal of money in a certain year. If, besides the profit made, he cashed the dividends of the shares he owns, declared everything in his income-tax return, he would have to pay a very high tax. But if he waited and collected the dividends of his shares in a lean year, he would have much less income tax to pay.

Presumably also, the able and cautious Vatican financiers, knowing that the exemption from the *cedolare* tax was still very much in the air, have preferred, in order not to scare Parliament and public opinion with the magnitude of the exemption obtained, to play it quietly. But this is of course merely a supposition.

Personally, and also going by the important and widespread positions held by Vatican lay financiers such as Spada, Pesenti, Galeazzi, Gualdi, the Pacelli brothers, Mennini, Sacchetti and the rest in the area of Italian banking, insurance, finance, investment, real estate, public works, public utilities, building and industry, I would say that the figure of 100 billion lire is an underestimate.

What is more important to consider is that the Vatican does not own only private shares but also a large amount of State bonds and debentures (*titoli* and *obbligazioni*), usually yielding between 5 per cent and 6 per cent, which are completely exempt from any form of taxation and which, being anonymous, escape any form of control as to their ownership. The same applies to debentures issued by State-controlled agencies, like IRI, ENI, ENEL, etc. And knowing the traditional caution of Vatican financiers, one can presume that the capital invested in State securities is larger than that invested in private shares.

These figures do not take into account the value of real estate, which is enormous. Although the Vatican is not likely to sell the Lateran Palace or the Cancelleria, it still has many buildings with shops and rented apartments which bring in quite a good income. Furthermore, it owns several thousand hectares of land, mostly near Rome and which, because of the rapid expansion of the city, comprises some very valuable building sites.

Another interesting aspect of the figures revealed by Finance Minister Preti is that the most important Vatican financial offices, as far as investments in Italy go, are not the Special Administration nor the Administration of the Holy See Patrimony, as commonly believed and often written, but the Institute for Religious Works. But it should also be noted that the Institute administers not only funds belonging to the Holy See in the strict meaning of the word, but also funds belonging to religious orders, to Vatican citizens who deposit their money in their private capacity, to foreign diplomats accredited to the Holy See and to a few privileged Italian businessmen.

All this, of course, leaves out Vatican investments outside Italy. This is a track much more difficult to follow, as the men holding important posts in the banking and industrial fields of each country are not so easily identifiable. We know that the Vatican has ties with the Rothschilds, the Crédit Suisse in Geneva, with Hambros Bank in London, with the Morgan Bank and the Bankers Trust Company in New York. It is also known that the Holy See has a considerable gold reserve which, however, is not kept in the Vatican but in Fort Knox. I have also been told that the Vatican owns the controlling shares in a Dutch company making nitrogen and in the Vienna company Poltzer making cellulose. But I have no proof.

A Yugoslav Communist, Frane Barbieri, who wrote a book about the financial and the political power of the Roman Church, listed a dozen banks in France and Luxembourg which he claimed belonged to the Vatican or to the Jesuits, but here again I could find no confirmation and I am therefore leaving them out. One should be very careful in these matters and neither underestimate nor overestimate the wealth of the Vatican.

As all things are relative, let us put the question in another and perhaps more sensible way. Is the Church of Rome rich or poor in relation to the tasks she has to perform? In this respect I would quote the words spoken by Pope Paul on 24 June 1965, in a speech he addressed to the College of Cardinals:

We shall say nothing here of other numerous and important extraordinary questions of an administrative nature, which keep the relevant offices alert and busy, like the radical and indispensable restoration of the Lateran Palace[1] or the projected

---

[1] The cost of which was $5 million.

building of a new hall for general audiences.[2] These questions, while making us feel the *blessed penury of our limited financial resources* (author's italics), should not distract us from the determination of multiplying as much as possible our relief to world hunger and our aid to the missionary, pastoral and charitable needs which are brought to our attention from so many parts. . . . We are encouraged by the signs of piety and generosity of so many of our sons who are determined not to let the charity of the Church lack the temporal means which prove her heart and make her hand beneficent.

I would put it this way. The Church of Rome is enormously rich but the tasks she is called on to perform are correspondingly prodigious, as the next chapter on Propaganda Fide will show more clearly. To talk about the 'blessed penury of our limited financial resources' tends to give the lie to the pomp that surrounds the Pope himself and the standard of life of Cardinals and Curia officials. Compared to Christ and his Apostles, they are all as rich as Croesus. But if one takes the Catholic Church as a whole on the level of the missionary, or of the humble parish priest, of monks, friars and nuns, then one could agree with the Pope and add that the Catholic Church manages to do a great deal with comparatively little.

[2] This is being built by Italy's best-known architect, Luigi Nervi. It will cost much more than the restoration of the Lateran Palace, and is not strictly necessary, as all previous Popes have managed without.

10

Propaganda Fide

Two thousand years have gone by since the birth of Christ and Adam's children have risen to over three billion. But still Christ's message has been accepted by only a quarter of humanity. The world population has increased more in the half-century from 1900 to 1950 than in the preceding eighteen centuries of the Christian era.

The population explosion, which is probably as dangerous as atomic weapons, still goes on. Dr B. R. Sen, until recently Director-General of FAO, wrote : 'If global war is averted we still face the problem of population growth which will double man's numbers by the end of the century. Today world population is increasing by about one and a quarter million people per week and most of them are born in the impoverished, inadequate-diet areas of the world and relatively fewer in the more prosperous areas where feeding, clothing and housing them is not the prime problem.'

We shall add that most of them are being born in non-Christian countries or where Christians are in a minority : Red China, India, Africa, Russia, the Arab countries and the South Pacific. Latin America, where the rate of growth is the highest, although it is Catholic on paper, is getting more and more de-Christianized. In Africa during the last thirty years an average of six million people a year were converted to Catholicism and about as many to Protestantism. But in the same period twenty-four million Africans embraced the Moslem faith every year. If the present trend continues, there will be much less than one Christian in four in the twenty-first century.

The arduous, desperate task of stopping and possibly reversing the trend is entrusted to the missionaries, who, in conditions always difficult and often dangerous, preach, teach, work and look after the sick and the starving.

Our scope is not that of telling the complex and moving story of the missionaries, but to examine how this operation is financed and controlled at headquarters, that is by the Congregation of Propaganda Fide in Rome. However, to give the reader an idea of the magnitude of the problem, I have recapitulated the more significant data, first divided by continents and then added up. They have been extracted from the Pontifical Yearbook and can therefore be considered official. The figures of the inhabitants do not correspond to the actual population of each continent, but to the inhabitants of the dioceses depending from Propaganda Fide.

Europe

Inhabitants: 24,706,185
Catholics: 916,747
Number of dioceses: 15
Diocesan priests: 338
Nuns: 2,125
Schools: 40
Students: 8,661
Relief agencies: 125

Seminarians: 158
Regular priests: 538
New priests[1]*:* 22
Male religious: 626
People assisted: 20,781
Hospitals: 37
Patients: 2,589

Note : in Europe the only countries and territories coming under Propaganda Fide are Scandinavia, North Albania, part of Yugoslavia and Gibraltar.

America

Inhabitants: 5,730,363
Catholics: 1,840,093
Number of dioceses: 14
Diocesan priests: 217
Seminarians: 104
Regular priests: 694
New priests: 14
Male religious: 681

Nuns: 2,221
Schools: 762
Students: 239,750
Relief agencies: 81
People assisted: 5,942
Hospitals: 87
Patients: 16,213

Note : in America the mission lands are Labrador, the North of Canada, including the Arctic, and the Antilles. The whole of Latin America is an exception being at the same time mission land and

[1] Ordained in the previous year.

having its own hierarchy which depends from the Congregation of the Bishops and the Congregation of the Clergy. Officially, out of nearly two hundred million Latin Americans, 175 million are Catholics. In practice in many regions the only sacrament that the majority of the people receive is baptism. The shortage of priests is terrible, the overall rate being one priest to 4,500 faithful. In the Antilles, if we exclude the priests not in charge of soul, the rate is of one to 18,000. This is why Latin America is partly considered to be a mission land.

Asia

Inhabitants: 1,076,766,184	*Nuns:* 44,371
Catholics: 15,952,163	*Schools:* 15,120
Number of dioceses: 300	*Students:* 3,583,954
Diocesan priests: 9,690	*Relief agencies:* 1,791
Seminarians: 4,136	*People assisted:* 385,954
Regular priests: 8,368	*Hospitals:* 1,408
New priests: 591	*Patients:* 2,157,117
Male religious: 10,947	

Note : the most populated continent—which includes Red China, India, Indonesia, Japan and Pakistan—is the one in which the Catholic Church is at its weakest. The rate of fifteen Catholics to 1,000 inhabitants revealed by our statistics would become even lower if one included vast areas of Red China from where missionaries have been completely banned and which do not appear in the Pontifical Yearbook.

Africa

Inhabitants: 163,074,085	*Nuns:* 23,701
Catholics: 24,844,163	*Schools:* 47,769
Number of dioceses: 236	*Students:* 4,276,226
Diocesan priests: 3,353	*Relief agencies:* 912
Seminarians: 1,901	*People assisted:* 2,418,184
Regular priests: 9,100	*Hospitals:* 4,494
Newly ordained priests: 252	*Patients:* 2,183,024
Male religious: 6,889	

Note : Africa as a whole, and leaving aside the higher conversion rate of the Moslems, appears to be the most promising hunting ground for both Catholic and Protestant missionaries. However, adding up the number of Africans attending Catholic schools (where they are also usually fed) and those receiving relief or medical care, we find that about ten out of twenty-four million gain some material advantages out of conversion.

Oceania

Inhabitants: 16,914,125
Catholics: 3,254,244
Number of dioceses: 45
Diocesan priests: 2,947
Seminarians: 1,330
Regular priests: 2,031
Newly ordained priests: 119
Male religious: 4,026

Nuns: 23,932
Schools: 2,997
Students: 618,521
Relief agencies: 374
People assisted: 109,036
Hospitals: 121
Patients: 38,871

Note : the statistics also include Australia and New Zealand. Actually these two countries long ago established their own hierarchies and continue to depend on Propaganda Fide only formally, because of tradition.

Whole World

Inhabitants: 1,256,754,394
Catholics: 46,870,410
Number of dioceses: 610
Diocesan priests: 16,545
Seminarians: 7,629
Regular priests: 20,731
Newly ordained priests: 998
Male religious: 23,169

Nuns: 96,350
Schools: 66,688
Students: 8,727,112
Relief agencies: 3,283
People assisted: 2,939,897
Hospitals: 6,147
Patients: 4,397,814

As one can infer from the above figures, the work done by the missionaries is all-embracing. But where does all the money come from? Mostly from donations by private people collected by four societies controlled by Propaganda Fide. In this respect one should note that the Catholic Church owes a special debt of gratitude to

France as far as fund-raising is concerned. Not only was the habit of collecting Peter's Pence revived in France by Count de Montalembert, but three of the four fund-raising societies controlled by Propaganda Fide were born in that country—two of them started by women.

The oldest and most important, the Pontifical Society for the Propagation of the Faith, was founded on 3 May 1822, by a group of Catholics from Lyon headed by a young French girl, Pauline Jaricot.

The ordinary members pay a small sum every year, which varies from country to country, and undertake to recite every day one paternoster and one Ave followed by the invocation : 'St Francis Xavier, pray for us'. The perpetual members pay a lump sum once and for all. Both ordinary and perpetual members enjoy plenary and partial indulgences granted to the society by various Popes. The society accepts all kinds of donations : money, real estate, precious objects, ancient coins, legacies, etc. In 1922 the headquarters were transferred to Rome. By then the society was well established all over the world.

In 1966 the society collected $27,152,365, which was $2,273,685 more than in the previous year. The funds collected have been steadily rising, except for the interruption of the war years. In 1960 the collection amounted to $20,428,565 and rose to $22,469,837 in 1961. The General Superior Council of the Society discloses every year the total amount collected but does not usually give a breakdown of the countries concerned. The general pattern, however, is that published in the magazine *Clero e missioni* (Clergy and missions) in October 1962 and which referred to the year 1961.

United States of America	$11,539,956
West Germany	$2,775,956
Italy	$1,127,200
France	$987,750
Canada	$842,935
Spain	$827,365
Holland	$622,421
Belgium	$570,000
Austria	$371,347
Australia	$317,128
Colombia	$293,044
Eire	$292,910
England	$229,600

As we can see the United States alone contributed more than all the other countries put together, while West Germany was second. This also happened, I was told by Propaganda Fide officials, in the subsequent years and it can be noted again not only in regard to the Society for the Propagation of the Faith but to fund-raising for the Catholic Church in general. Germany, as we shall see later, is an exception as she contributes vast amounts of money through other channels, and is far from being as outdistanced by the USA as it would appear from the figures above.

The then general-secretary of the society, Mgr Raymond Etteldorf, who is now Apostolic Delegate in New Zealand, explained how this organization works:

> The Society is organized first on a diocesan level. The funds collected through the Society in each diocese are sent by the diocesan director to the national director, who in turn reports the total amount collected each year in his country to the Superior Council of the Pontifical Society for the Propagation of the Faith in Rome. According to the statutes of the society, the Superior Council is solely authorized to distribute its funds to the missions. Hence, the allocation of the money that is collected for the missions is made by the same organization to which it is given.
>
> The Superior Council is made up of the national directors and of priests and prelates representing their countries in

Rome : two from France, where the Society was founded, and one from each of the following countries : Belgium, Brazil, Canada, England, Germany, Scotland, Holland, Ireland, Italy, Mexico, Spain, Switzerland and the United States of America. The Superior Council meets three times a year to decide on the allocation of the funds to the missions in various parts of the world.

None of the money is invested in banks for long-term interest; whatever is given to the Society is distributed to the missions within a year from the time that it is received by the Superior Council. The cost of the administration by the secretariat of the Superior Council last year amounted to 0.16 per cent, or notably less than one per cent, of the total income.

The subsidies distributed to the missions are divided into two categories : ordinary and extraordinary. There are 793 dioceses or ecclesiastical circumscriptions that are eligible for aid, and each of these receives an ordinary subsidy towards its maintenance.

Every missionary in the territory that comes under Propaganda Fide may make a request for financial aid for a special project, such as the construction of a church, a school, a hospital, an orphanage, a leprosarium, or for the training and support of catechists. Every legitimate request, approved by or coming from the local authorities, is presented to the Superior Council at its meeting and a grant, known as an extraordinary subsidy, is made in proportion to the funds available.

You may have noticed that there is a considerable discrepancy between the figure of 793 dioceses or ecclesiastical circumscriptions mentioned by Mgr Etteldorf and the figure of 610 dioceses I quoted in my statistics taken from the Pontifical Yearbook 1967. The fact is that we were, I hope, both right. He included the dioceses of the Oriental Churches which, although not controlled by Propaganda Fide receive subsidies from the Superior Council of the Pontifical Society for the Propagation of the Faith, while I, to simplify matters, left them out.

Two French women, Stephanie Cottin and her daughter Jeanne Bigard of Caen, founded in 1889 the Society of St Peter the Apostle with the object of contributing to the training of the native clergy of the missions. It is an extremely important task, as the Church of Rome can never hope to influence coloured people by using only white missionaries. It is even more important today, when anti-colonialism and the national pride of countries that have recently acquired independence are flourishing, than it was when the society was founded. Also this organization was promoted to the rank of Pontifical and its headquarters moved to Rome under the supervision of Propaganda Fide.

The members undertake to pay for the keep and the studies of one native seminarian every year, or contribute a lump sum to cover the six-year curriculum of a seminarian. In this case there is a form of complete 'adoption'. Otherwise several benefactors can form a group to share the expense of keeping and training a seminarian. The benefactors receive a photograph of the seminarian and reports concerning his life and studies.

In 1965 the society had at its disposal $9,839,578, half of which had been collected among the members and half produced by the Society for the Propagation of the Faith. In 1967 the total amount of subsidies distributed by the society had risen to $11,155,804. They were divided as follows :—

a) *Ordinary subsidies for the maintenance of seminaries:*

Africa :	$2,988,487
Asia :	$2,199,459
America :	$353,210
Oceania :	$105,400
Europe :	$35,960

b) *Extraordinary subsidies for enlargements of buildings:*

Africa :	$3,013,020
Asia :	$1,574,496
America :	$480,400
Oceania :	$218,500
Europe :	$187,872

c) *Grand total:*

Ordinary subsidies	$5,682,516
Extraordinary subsidies	$5,474,388
Total	$11,156,904

The third organization for raising funds for the missions was founded in 1843 by another Frenchman, Mgr Auguste de Forbin-Janson, bishop of Nancy. It is called the Pontifical Society for the Holy Childhood and its original object was to help Chinese children. Now it assists children in all the mission lands. Everything in this society is on a small scale: its protector is the Infant Jesus, its members are children below 12 years of age, their undertaking is to say every day an Ave Maria followed by the prayer: 'Virgin Mary, St Joseph, pray for us and for the little infidel children'. At the end of each month the members are expected to give a small contribution.

Despite these modest premises, the society collected in 1966 no less than 40,861,554 French francs with an increase of 1,795,377 francs over the previous year. Compared with 1960, fund-raising has increased by 47 per cent. The largest increase was made in the USA, West Germany, Italy, Spain and Ireland. The headquarters are in Paris, 12 boulevard Flandrin, Paris 16°. The president is Mgr Adrien Bressolles. The funds collected are sent to Propaganda Fide and redistributed among the missions.

The fourth and last society collecting funds for the missions and controlled by Propaganda Fide is the Missionary Union of the Clergy. It was founded in 1908 by the Italian Father Paolo Manna, of the Foreign Missions of Milan, to collect money from priests all over the world. In 1957 Pius XII promoted it to Pontifical Society and extended the membership to the religious, seminarists and nuns. No figures are disclosed, partly because of a technical reason, inasmuch as the sums collected are not sent to Propaganda Fide in Rome but dispensed among the missions by local hierarchies, and possibly also because one doesn't want to establish a comparison between the generosity of laymen and that of the clerics. However, the main object of the union is more spiritual than financial; prayers, the encouragement of vocations, preaching, informing the faithful and stimulating their interest in the missions. It has about 250,000 members.

The Congregation of Propaganda Fide, as we saw in the previous chapter, also has some funds of its own invested in Italian shares. Only a negligible quantity. The backbone of its finances are the four societies mentioned above which collect money from laymen, clerics, children scattered all over the world and re-distribute them among the missions of Asia, Africa, America, Oceania and Europe.

The head of the Congregation, also known as the Red Pope[2] because of the colour of his robes and of the blood that his legions are often called upon to shed, is Cardinal Gregory Peter Agagianian, a seventy-five-year-old bearded Armenian, born not far away from Stalin's native village, but who studied as a seminarist in Rome and has become Italianized.

There is a committee of no less than thirty-nine Cardinals, all of equal standing. The secretary is the recently appointed, up-and-coming Bishop Sergio Pignedoli, strongly backed by Pope Paul. Prince Carlo Pacelli is legal adviser to the Congregation and Prince Giulio Pacelli is the legal procurator.

Apart from the four fund-raising organizations we have examined, and which constitute the backbone of Propaganda Fide's finances, there are countless other independent rivers and rivulets that flow into the vast reservoir of charity for the support of missionaries. Added together, these independent contributions exceed by far the financial means at the disposal of the Roman congregation. In other words, should the Catholic missionaries have to rely entirely on the money they get from Rome, most of them would find it extremely difficult, if not impossible, to operate.

It would be too involved and also outside the scope of this book to try and keep track of all channels through which Catholic missions receive help. But one cannot avoid mentioning the truly splendid effort produced by two West German Catholic organizations which were born after the war: Misereor and Adveniat. In 1966 these two comparatively recent organizations collected in West Germany alone 104 million marks, that is nearly $25 million. A figure that compares very favourably with the $27 million collected in the same year by the Pontifical Society for the Propagation of the Faith all over the world, including the USA and West Germany.

To be more exact, in 1966 Misereor, which dedicates its efforts to Africa, collected 56 million marks, which brought the total amount collected since 1956 to 330 million. Adveniat, which 'specializes' in Latin America, collected over 48 million marks. They both bypass Propaganda Fide and instead of spreading their money evenly (for instance, assigning a certain sum to each of the 236

[2] The Pope himself is the *White Pope* and the General of the Jesuits is known as the *Black Pope*.

African dioceses in proportion to population), they finance specific projects they themselves supervise. They want to know exactly where their money goes.

Let us take, as an example of how the operation works, what Adveniat did in Latin America in 1966. This organization, which was founded seven years ago, collects funds, as its name indicates, during the period of the Advent, that is, before Christmas. The 1966 collection brought in exactly 48,282,399 marks, which was 6.22 per cent more than the preceding year. The main theme of their Latin-American campaign for that year was that of unity, not only in the religious but also in the social sense. The union of the peasants to promote self-help and the union of labour movements; the banding together of the inhabitants of the slums which so often surround the big Latin-American cities to help them 'to transform their huts into houses and their superstition into faith'; the union of intellectuals and students; and the union of teachers, both ecclesiastic and lay.

The largest sum (8,812,662 marks) was used for the instruction and the apostolate of laymen, including the building of institutes for the training of catechists, and salaries for teachers of religion. 6,945,241 marks were allocated for pastoral work and social reforms, which included financing episcopal conferences and spreading the social doctrine of the Church, especially the *Populorum progressio* which seems to be ideally suited to Latin America. At parish level Adveniat spent in Latin America 5,257,248 marks to build parishes, repair churches and give financial assistance to priests and social workers. 5,045,920 marks were spent on schools of various types, from elementary schools to theological faculties. The pastoral assistance to students (building special centres, boarding schools, subsidizing chaplains, etc.) absorbed 3,063,900 marks. Newspapers, magazines, radio and television stations, and special courses for the training of journalists took 2,749,623 marks. It is a sizeable sum of money, and precisely 2,414,650 was spent on means of transport : automobiles, small aeroplanes to cover the enormous distances of Latin America, jeeps, river boats and motorized chapels. DM 1,852,140 were spent to help female religious orders and 1,653,200 on seminaries. The remaining 10,487,815 were allotted to various projects under study and to assist old or sick priests.

Adveniat apart, the Catholics of West Germany are also making a considerable contribution to Latin America through the 'twinning' of German and Latin-American dioceses. For instance, in the period from 1 July 1966 to 31 July 1967, they set aside 7,982,922 marks to give scholarships to future priests, which corresponded to a monthly subsidy of 50 marks for each seminarist.

Nor can one help mentioning, although it is not directly concerned with missionary lands but to the world in general, the achievements of the USA Catholic Relief Service. It has been made known that in the fiscal year ending on 30 June 1967, this organization carried out in seventy different countries a programme of relief and development valued at $157.3 million. The USA Government provided the bulk of the relief with surplus agricultural commodities worth $77.6 million and also paid 19.2 million in ocean freight reimbursements. 35 million came from the Bishops' Thanksgiving Clothing Collection, 9.1 million from the National Council of Catholic Women and 9.3 million from other sources. The countries that received more help were Vietnam (16.1 million), Brazil (13.3 million) and India (12.6 million).

The Vatican, of course, views these activities with gratitude and praise, but also nurses some misgivings about them, especially where Misereor and Adveniat are concerned. There are two reasons for this : the first is the fear that central authority might be weakened by what are described in the Vatican as 'private' activities; the second is that certain mission areas may be favoured more than others. I shall quote in this respect what the Belgian Jesuit Father J. Masson, Maître de Conférences at the University of Louvain, wrote in his comment on the decree on missionary activity approved by the Ecumenical Council.[3]

> One must establish a right balance, definitely vertical, between the pontifical missionary societies and the private societies. It is not a question of suppressing the latter as the Popes have often reiterated, but they have also underlined more and more the priority of the pontifical missionary societies. Why have these directions been issued? Because, although private societies and direct contacts established by the missionaries do undoubtedly personalize and develop the interest of Christians in the missions, there is also the danger of fierce competition

[3] *Le missioni nel Vaticano II* Elle Ci Di (Turin, 1966).

through rival propaganda and of a monopoly in the allotment of the funds collected. The groups that ask for more help are not always necessarily the most needy. . . . It is therefore necessary that a disinterested superior authority should have priority in receiving from the Christians the fundamental and main resources, which it will then use according to a universal vision of the *more urgent* necessities in the *most appropriate* areas. Private initiative is not always capable of discerning rightly these necessities and these areas.

Similar misgivings held for similar reasons are expressed in Vatican quarters also about the spreading habit of 'twinning' prosperous European dioceses with missionary dioceses, like those that have been established between Cologne and Tokyo, Milan and Rhodesia, Treviso in Italy and Sangmélima in Africa, Lieges-Nyundo, Lilles-Cameroon, between certain dioceses in the Basque province and others in Latin America, etc.

But leaving aside this not too crucial problem, I would conclude this necessarily brief outline of the vast and complex activities of Propaganda Fide with the remark that it is a sector of the Church of Rome which, from the financial point of view, is the least clouded in secrecy. Up to a certain point, one can find out where the money comes from and where it goes to.

11

Cardinal Moneybags

Whenever a new Cardinal is appointed and whatever his nationality, a Roman church is assigned to him, the so-called titular church. It is an ancient custom which symbolizes the fact that, however alien his origin and however far away his See may lie, Rome is his spiritual home. Titular churches are often assigned according to their connections with the new Cardinal's country of origin. Thus it is quite natural that the church of St Sylvester, which is the English church of Rome, should have been given to the English Cardinal Heenan and that the church of St Susanna, which is the American church, should have been assigned to Cardinal Cushing, Archbishop of Boston.

But there is also another more subtle criterion, of a financial character, by which the titular churches are distributed; the poorer the church, the richer the Cardinal. In this context, 'rich' does not refer to the Cardinal's personal wealth, but to the wealth of his diocese. The idea is to assign the churches that are badly in need of repair, or which are out of the way and therefore have small congregations (and meagre collections) and those situated in poor districts, to Cardinals who have sufficient means to repair them, restore them and often embellish them.

When the late Francis Spellman, Archbishop of New York, who died in December 1967, was made a Cardinal by Pope Pius XII in February 1946, he was given as titular church the beautiful but ruinous church of St John and St Paul, on the Celio hill. The façade of this church, which is one of the best examples of the Romanesque style, has since been freed from later additions and, through a painstaking, long and very costly work of restoration, brought back to its pure and simple lines. Excavations under the floor of the church, which involved considerable technical problems, have been completed, revealing a very interesting ancient Roman house in which, according to a rather shaky tradition, St Paul himself is said to have lived.

The name of Cardinal Spellman has already been mentioned in the course of our narrative. But he deserves more attention, not only because of his remarkable personality but also because he was a clever financier, and through him we shall be able to see how the richest diocese in the world, that of New York, was administered.

Spellman was born in Whitman, a small manufacturing town in Massachusetts, on 4 May 1889, into a family of second-generation Americans of Irish descent. Francis was the first-born of five children. The father, William Spellman, was a grocer and Francis, while attending grammar school and then the public high school, helped his father in the shop. Like all Americans who made good, he delivered newspapers from house to house and worked during the holidays. For a few months he drove a local trolley.

He then went to the Fordham University in New York where, besides studying with more zeal than brilliance, he wrote poetry and articles for the *Fordham Monthly*, took part in debates and joined a scientific society of undergraduates. He felt the call of the Church during his last year of university and, after having passed an examination, he was admitted to the North American College in Rome.

After five years Spellman was ordained (1916) and sent to Boston to work as assistant to the parish priest of a small church in Roxburg. Two years later the formidable and despotic archbishop of Boston, Cardinal William O'Connell, made him assistant to the chancellor of the archdiocese and Spellman thus acquired his first taste of financial problems. Subsequently he fell out of favour with the Cardinal and might have ended his career as an obscure priest in Boston had it not been for a curious incident.

During the 1925 Holy Year a pilgrimage from Boston went to Rome headed by a bishop who could speak very little Italian. Spellman was assigned to him as an interpreter. Pope Pius XI received the pilgrims and spoke to them for a quarter of an hour— in Italian. The bishop then attempted a translation, which amounted to a few stilted phrases of welcome. The Pope was somewhat surprised by the drastic way in which his speech had been condensed, but made no comment.

Mgr Francesco Borgongini-Duca, later a Cardinal, who had been

Spellman's teacher while the latter was in Rome as a seminarist, had watched the scene with amusement. A few days later, when the Pope spoke again to a group of Americans, he asked his former pupil Spellman to translate. This time the translation lasted slightly longer than the original speech. Pius XI, who did not speak English but understood it, was very impressed by the way Spellman had remembered everything he had said and by the clearness and eloquence with which he had reproduced his thoughts. A few months later Spellman was recalled from Boston and given a job in the Secretariat of State under the famous Cardinal Pietro Gasparri. He was the first American to join the State Secretariat, traditionally in the hands of Italians.

In 1929, after the signing of the Concordat with Italy, Cardinal Gasparri retired to private life and his place was taken by Cardinal Eugenio Pacelli, former Nuncio in Munich and the future Pope Pius XII. A firm friendship developed between the tall, pale ascetic Italian aristocrat and the plump, round-faced, rosy-cheeked, jovial and pragmatic American prelate, a friendship that was to continue when Pacelli became Pope.

In 1932, having spent seven years in the State Secretariat, Spellman was consecrated bishop and sent back to Boston. Pius XI had intended to appoint him bishop-coadjutor of Cardinal O'Connell, who was getting on in years, which would have been the equivalent of designating him as O'Connell's successor. But O'Connell put his foot down and Spellman had to be content with the minor rank of auxiliary bishop. Another seven years went by and in September 1938 the archbishop of New York, Cardinal Hayes, died. The appointment of a successor was delayed and in February of the next year Pius XI also died. He was succeeded by Pacelli who, in April 1939, nominated his old friend Spellman Archbishop of New York and in 1946 gave him the red hat.

The appointment came as a surprise and a shock to the clergy of New York who had expected and hoped that one of their own bishops would have been promoted. The new archbishop was received rather coldly. But soon his energy, his practical sense, his cordial and relaxed manners and his talent for making friends changed this. Not only did the New York clergy start referring to him as 'Spelly', but he became a leading figure in American public life, the friend of presidents, of generals, of Jewish financiers and of tough union leaders alike.

When Spellman took over, the archdiocese of New York was in financial straits. The depression had left its mark and most of the churches, schools, convents, monasteries, hospitals and other buildings housing Catholic institutions were heavily mortgaged. The total debt of the archdiocese amounted to about $28 million.

For the first few months Spellman studied the situation, then he started what was to become an habitual procedure. He asked bankers, financiers and businessmen to lunch. In this way he was able to gather useful information and to prepare a plan of action. His first bold move was to wipe out all the mortgages of the various parishes. The idea was very simple. He had discovered that, while the parishes paid an interest of 5 per cent to 6.5 per cent on the mortgages, he could have borrowed money paying only 2 per cent on five year loans and 2.5 per cent on ten year loans. The immediate saving was of at least $\frac{1}{2}$ million. Another consequence was that the archdiocese became the central bank for all the parishes which, before Spellman, had had entirely separate administrations.

He then applied the same principle of a unified administration to practically all the transactions in which the parishes were hitherto engaged independently. The idea was again very simple : it was easier to negotiate and obtain better terms if he operated on a big scale, from a position of strength with the entire financial power of the archdiocese behind him, rather than allow the parish priests to do their own bargaining in a scattered and often amateurish way. For example, it was much cheaper to buy in bulk all the candles needed in the various Catholic churches in New York than to let the parish priests do their individual and sporadic buying. Today all the buying for the New York archdiocese, from the candles we mentioned above to the six thousand automobiles in use, from the wine for the Mass to all the furniture for the various schools, hospitals, convents, etc., is done by a staff of about fifty people and it saves about $1 million a year on an expenditure of $14 million.

But one can quote a much more flamboyant and convincing example of Spellman's financial genius. In 1947 the American building industry had not yet fully recovered from the post-war slump. Spellman realized that the big building firms were eager to start working again on a big scale, but also that prices were not likely to drop because of the high wages the unions were determined to get. On the other hand, he had an ambitious building programme to carry out. He knew that there must be some way to take advantage of the situation and that, if building costs were high, at least one should try to buy the best possible quality of work at a reasonable price.

In an after-lunch speech delivered at the Hotel Astor to the presidents of the biggest construction firms of New York and to the top leaders of the building unions, Spellman outlined his building programme and stated that, as a start, he was ready to pay out $25 million immediately. An appealing figure, even for a city as big as New York, and especially during a building slump. Both contractors and trade unionists pricked up their ears. The Cardinal then added : 'All I need to launch this programme are two guarantees : from the construction companies a good job for the price; and from labour a good day's work for the pay.' He was cheered by all sides and within a few days the first contracts were being signed.

After that Cardinal Spellman embarked on almost feverish building activity which was second only to that of the municipality of New York. Among his most impressive achievements is the reconstructed Foundling Hospital on Lexington Avenue which has room for three hundred children and which cost $12 million, and the 'Aloysius Stepinac' high school in White Plains which cost $5 million and takes 1,600 pupils. It has been reckoned that every year he was responsible for construction worth about $90 million. To be specific, Cardinal Spellman, up to 1964, had built 130 new schools, thirty-seven churches and five big hospitals.

One of his most sensational and profitable coups was the purchase in 1952 (from the heirs of Whitelaw Reid, for a mere $400,000) of 250 acres of land which constituted the Reid country estate, Ophir Hall, Purchase, New York. The Cardinal installed on it, at the cost of $15 million, the Manhattanville College of the Sacred Heart, which houses about seven hundred girls and which used to be in upper Manhattan. By selling to the city the old site of the college Spellman recouped $8,800,000.

No small wonder that the following joke should be told about

Cardinal Spellman. Having died, he knocks at the gate of Heaven asking for admission.

'Who are you?' enquires St Peter.

'A humble priest from New York, the name is Spellman.'

'Hold on a minute,' St Peter says, keeping the gate closed, 'let me check on our list.' He returns a little later and adds : 'Sorry, but we cannot find your name. Could you give me some more details?'

'Well,' Spellman answers, a little annoyed, 'I was the Archbishop of New York and in charge of all the chaplains in the USA armed forces, if that rings a bell.'

Again St Peter disappears and returns shaking his head.

'But I'm Francis Cardinal Spellman. You must have heard of me!'

'All right, I'll check again,' says St Peter patiently. When he returns for the third time, he flings the gate wide open and beams.

'Come right in, Frank, old boy. I'm sorry about this delay. But, you see, we had you under real estate.'

Anyhow, not even with Spellman's talent for business, with his policy of centralization and rationalization of diocesan finances, could New York have ever achieved the prominence it has today in the Catholic world, had it not been for the truly exceptional generosity of the New York Catholics. Clever business deals, sound finances, savings, even occasional lucky strikes in the real estate game, are all very well. But they could not have been carried through and sustained if there had not been a big and steady flow of private contributions.

It is interesting to note what New York Catholics succeeded in building, organizing and supporting under Spellman's leadership. However, the expression 'New York' can be misleading. One must not think, in our context, of New York as a city of over nine million inhabitants, but only of Spellman's former jurisdiction, which practically means reducing it by half.

The New York archdiocese for which Spellman was responsible included Manhattan, the Bronx, Richmond (Staten Island) in the city proper and beyond, Westchester, Putnam, Dutchess, Orange, Rockland, Sullivan and Ulster counties. It had, according to the 1967 Pontifical Yearbook from which the data that follow are derived, a population of 4,950,000 of which 1,651,400 are Catholics.

The other half of New York city is included in the diocese of Brooklyn, administered by Bishop Bryan Joseph McEntegart, with a population of 4,436,897 of which 1,585,712 are Catholics. From a purely numerical point of view, Bishop McEntegart's responsibility was almost equal to that of Spellman.

In the New York archdiocese the Catholics represent 33 per cent of the population. The rest is made of 28 per cent atheists (or rather people with no declared religious affiliation), 27 per cent Jews, while the remaining 12 per cent are mostly Protestants with a sprinkling of Moslems, Buddhists and other religions.

To get a more precise picture of the flock under the care of the New York Archbishop one should note that about 600,000 of the Catholics are Puerto Ricans—the poorest, the most recent and least integrated immigrants. They represent not only an ethnical but also a linguistic problem, which the Cardinal overcame by sending half of the newly ordained priests to the Caribbean for three months to learn some Spanish and get acquainted with the mentality of the people. From a financial point of view they are much more of a burden than an asset.

The other New York Catholics are mostly of Irish and Italian descent, two racial groups that have only recently begun to emerge from the lower strata of the population to prominent positions in business and public life. All told, not a very promising flock from a purely money-raising point of view. But as Manhattan contains probably the highest concentration of millionaires in the world, the Cardinal was able to more than overcome the handicap.

It is as well to remember that a large percentage of the contributors to Spellman's charities and collections were non-Catholics. When he gave his usual yearly luncheon party at the Waldorf Hotel, the 2,500 places costing $100 each were always overbooked and Protestants and Jews figured prominently among the guests.

Education no doubt represented the most striking feature of Spellman's achievements : 452 Catholic schools with the impressive attendance of 248,461 pupils in 1966. The Catholic hospitals numbered twenty-six with 5,456 patients and the charitable institutions thirty-five with 8,650 people assisted. From a strictly ecclesiastic point of view, there were 403 parishes, 1,261 diocesan priests, 1,273 regular priests, 221 seminarians, 26 newly ordained priests, 1,256 religious and 8,562 nuns.

What did it all cost and where did the money come from? Here again, as it so often happens where financial matters are concerned, the Church's rule of silence prevailed. A request for basic data addressed to Cardinal Spellman a few months before his death was totally ignored. However, an approximate reckoning of the expenses borne by the archdiocese plus the monies collected for charities and for the missions can give us a rough idea of the generosity of Cardinal Spellman's flock. According to an estimate made in 1964 by *Time* magazine, the Cardinal was then spending $90 million a year on construction. A detailed survey carried out in 1960 by the authoritative financial magazine *Fortune* estimated that Catholic charities absorbed $50 million a year and the Catholic schools $22 million. In this respect it should be noted that, by using nuns and brothers to teach instead of salaried lay teachers, the Catholic elementary schools spend $85 a year for each pupil against the $300 spent by the municipal elementary schools. There are then innumerable other smaller expenses, such as the upkeep of the churches, the stipends of the priests, the training of the seminarians, the running of convents and monasteries, etc., which were all financed by the contributions of the faithful.

Peter's Pence, which is usually collected on the third Sunday of January in all the New York churches, is reported to bring in about $1 million a year. We have already seen to what great extent the missionaries have to rely on contributions from the USA and we were unofficially told at Propaganda Fide that the archdiocese of Cardinal Spellman topped the list. The Cardinal was also engaged in collecting funds for the Catholic Relief Services. Here again the New York Catholics were ahead. All told, the estimate made by *Fortune* in 1960, according to which the annual revenues and collections of Spellman's archdiocese amounted to about $150 million, would today be on the conservative side and should be increased if referred to 1967.

It is therefore quite understandable that Cardinal Spellman should have been nicknamed in Rome, with a mixture of admiration and envy, 'Cardinal Moneybags' and that, whenever he paid a visit to Rome, there were whispers in the corridors of the Vatican :

'You know, Cardinal Moneybags has brought Peter's Pence to the Pope. Imagine : a cheque for $1 million !'

'Have you heard? Cardinal Moneybags has given over $1 million to finance the Ecumenical Council.'

He was not ashamed of his wealth and whenever he visited Rome he booked the royal suite at the Grand Hotel, whereas other Cardinals, in order to save money, usually stayed in homes run by nuns or friars. In this connection a curious episode took place a few years ago. Spellman had booked his usual suite at the Grand for a certain day at a time when President Soekarno of Indonesia was staying there. But as Soekarno was scheduled to leave Rome the day before Spellman's arrival, all appeared to be well. But suddenly Soekarno changed his mind. He had been introduced by Rome's top procuress to a couple of call girls whom he found particularly rewarding, had installed them in his apartment and decided to stay on two more days. Quite a commotion followed. The management insisted that Soekarno must leave the suite on the appointed day, Soekarno insisted on staying and suggested that the Cardinal should be accommodated elsewhere. Finally the management won, but only at the last moment.

A priest from Santa Susanna, the American Catholic Church in Rome, described the scene, 'There I was, standing in the corridor of the hotel, with a portable altar I had been instructed to install in the Cardinal's suite, while the staff were hastily removing to other rooms the belongings of Soekarno's call girls. I wasn't even quite sure that the girls themselves had been removed. I was nervously looking at my watch expecting "Spelly" to appear round the corner any minute. But we made it, just in time.'

All this, of course, is purely coincidental and it doesn't detract nor add to Spellman's figure. One might just note in passing that, if Soekarno had intended to stage a status showdown with Cardinal Spellman, he had certainly chosen the wrong hotel. For the Grand Hotel belongs to CIGA Compagnia Italiana Grandi Alberghi (capital 8 billion lire) in which the Vatican, as we have seen, has an interest and whose vice-president is Marquis Giacinto Guglielmi, one of the Vatican financiers.

Anyhow, episodes like this were related with glee in Vatican circles where they were never quite able to decide what to make of Cardinal Spellman. On one hand his habit of smoking large cigars in public, of slapping people on the back, of letting himself be photographed while playing tennis or swimming in the sea with a mother superior (this was several years ago), were considered eccentricities not worthy of a Prince of the Church, while on the other hand his organizing and financial ability and the splendid pastoral work he carried out commanded respect and admiration.

After the death of Pius XII and of John XXIII several American newspapers suggested that Spellman might have been elected Pope. To those cognizant of Vatican affairs these suggestions appeared preposterous. Not so much because of his back-slapping or cigar-smoking but, more consequently, because his close connection with Wall Street and his being also the head (*Vicario Castrense*) of all the chaplains of the USA armed forces, would have given the enemies of the Church too good an opportunity to identify the papacy with 'American capitalists and imperialists'.

    12

Kirchensteuer Über Alles

The object of this book has been to unravel, as far as possible, the
mystery of Vatican finances at central, top level. An exception was
the chapter on Cardinal Spellman. It is included for several reasons.
As it happened, not only was Spellman a very able and modern-
minded administrator, but he organized the richest Catholic diocese
in the world and induced his flock to contribute to the Church of
Rome more money than anybody else before him. I have also
chosen Cardinal Spellman as a symbol of the efficiency of the whole
Catholic hierarchy of the United States (not forgetting the generous
American laity) because, without the steady flow of dollars collected
in one form or another, neither the Vatican would be as relatively
well off as it is today, nor would Catholic missionaries in Africa,
Latin America, Asia and Oceania be able to carry on the considerable work they do. A second exception can be made for West
Germany, not only because this country is the second biggest source
of income of the Church of Rome, but also because of the rather
unusual situation that exists there.

From the financial point of view, the Catholic Church enjoys in
Germany an exceptional and privileged position. It need not worry
about how and where to find the funds necessary to face its needs
and commitments. The State looks after it by collecting the
Kirchensteuer (Church tax) from both Catholics and Protestants
alike and handing it over to the respective ecclesiastical authorities.

This tax has remote origins, but it found its constitutional basis
for the first time with the Weimar Constitution of 1919. It was
confirmed by the Concordat concluded in 1933, under the reign of
Pius XI, between the Holy See and Hitler's Reich. The Secretary
of State was at the time Cardinal Eugenio Pacelli, the future
Pius XII. Thus, while solicitor Francesco Pacelli was instrumental
in concluding the Concordat with Fascist Italy, his brother Eugenio

151

had a leading role in concluding that with Nazi Germany. The two brothers prepared the juridical instruments which, in conjunction with the rise and establishment of strong Catholic parties in the respective countries, constitute today very powerful assets for the Vatican. In Italy one could not introduce divorce without modifying the Concordat, in Germany one could not abolish the Kirchensteuer without doing the same. For while the Italian Concordat was embodied in the Constitution of 1947, the German Kirchensteuer was made constitutional by the Grundgesetz of 1949.

The amount of money that this tax on religion involves is truly remarkable. It has been reckoned by the authoritative German magazine *Capital,* from which we drew the data that follow, that the two main German confessions, the Catholic and the Protestant (Evangelisch), received in 1965 about DM 3.2 billion, of which no less than DM 2.8 billion came from the Kirchensteuer. To be more exact, the Protestant Church received DM 1.6 billion and the Catholics DM 1.2 billion. The Protestants got a bit more because they are more numerous (51 per cent Protestants against 44 per cent Catholics out of the entire population) and also because, on average, they are more affluent.

The church tax, however, represents a heavy burden on the German taxpayer : from 8 per cent to 10 per cent of income tax, according to the various Laender. Frankly one cannot imagine any Government in England, France, Italy, the USA, or even ultra-Catholic Spain, daring to impose such a stiff addition to income tax for the purpose of supporting religion. But Germans are used to it and seem to take it in their stride.

This is even more remarkable if one considers that church attendance and the practice of religion are rather limited in Germany and that the paying of the church tax is voluntary. According to Dr Norbert Greinacher, a well-known sociologist of Vienna University, quoted by *Capital,* German Catholics can be divided into four groups according to the intensity of their belief :

20 per cent are closely connected with the church
30 per cent attend religious functions regularly but have no close ties
40 per cent are marginal Catholics and attend seldom
10 per cent are unbelievers

The picture appears even grimmer if one consider the Protestants. It has been reckoned that in Bavaria and in Wuerttenberg only about 10 per cent attend church regularly, while in Hamburg attendance reaches only 2.5 per cent.

The church tax, as we have said, is voluntary, and only those who officially declare themselves to be either Catholics or Protestants are asked to pay it. The number of people who renounce their religion in order not to pay the tax is, however, limited : about 40,000 Protestants and 23,000 Catholics a year. Not very many, if compared with the annual increase of population and therefore of taxpayers.

How does one then explain these two contrasting factors, especially in the case of the Protestants : on the one hand church attendance, the practice of religion and the influence of religion on human behaviour are dwindling; while on the other hand the willingness to pay a rather heavy tax in favour of the church remains practically unchanged? One can think of several reasons and combine them together : tradition, conformism, the fear of losing status by renouncing one's religion for financial reasons, or of renouncing the celebration of marriages, baptisms, confirmations, funerals, with the solemnity that the church can provide. Last but not least, there may also be a vague feeling that religion, even if one does not practise it personally, is something good for others and an element of social stability.

Although the church tax paid by individuals in proportion to their incomes constitutes the bulk of the revenues of the Catholic and of the Evangelic churches, this is not the end of the story. Business companies too are made to pay a tax on profits in favour of the two confessions. The Arbeitsgemeinschaft Selbständiger Unternehmer (ASU)[1] has for several years protested against this burden and its unequal division. The ASU pointed out, for instance, that a registered company had to pay DM 80,000 for the Kirchen-steuer, while had it been a limited company it would have had to pay only DM 2,500. And Professor Günter Schmölders of Cologne, a financial expert, has reckoned that in Nordrhein-Westfalen the 3.4 per cent of Protestants subjected to the tax paid as much as 54.7 per cent of the total in 1961.

[1] This is a permanent committee created by independent businessmen to study their problems and defend their interests.

In several Catholic dioceses a percentage of taxes paid on land or on patrimony (Vermoegenssteuer) also goes to the church. And in certain Laender Catholics who are exempted from income tax because they are too poor, are old age pensioners or have many children, still have to pay a yearly tribute to the church which varies from DM 4 to 60.

Another big advantage offered by the Christian Democrat Government of Bonne to the two churches was the collection of the tax by the State machinery. The Government collects the tax, enforces its payment in case of defaulting and deducts only between 3 per cent and 4 per cent for expenses before handing the money over to the church authorities. In the days of the Weimar Republic and of the Nazi regime the Catholic and the Protestant Churches had to do their own tax collecting, which meant sometimes having to resort to court action. The new system, besides being more convenient, is also much cheaper. 'If we had to collect the tax ourselves,' a prelate of the archdiocese of Cologne admitted, 'it would cost us at least 10 per cent of the amount collected.'

But what does the church tax mean in personal terms? Before 1945 the Germans used to pay up on average 2 or 3 marks a year for their respective churches. Today, with devaluation, the economic boom and various other circumstances, the figure has risen to the considerable level of DM 55 a year per person, which, in wealthy cities like Duesseldorf, can reach an average of DM 110. Besides the church tax and the other payments mentioned above, the State, the Laender and the communes contribute another DM 250 million a year to the two confessions for building, teaching, public relief programmes, etc. All told, the two churches derive from the civil authorities—in the end, that is, from the taxpayers—about 90 per cent of their total revenues.

This evidence may justify the initial statement that the Catholic Church enjoys a very special and privileged position in West Germany. To have 90 per cent of one's very considerable income guaranteed, collected and automatically delivered by the civil authorities is an asset that no other Catholic community in the world can boast of.[2]

[2] In Spain the Government contributes about 50 per cent of Catholic Church expenditure, but there is no church tax and the contribution is voluntary.

Paradoxically the Catholic Church owes this privileged position to two of her worst enemies: Luther and Napoleon. For the juridical justification of all the money the Catholic Church collects today from the German State is based on the loss of church property suffered because of Luther's Reformation and because of the high-handed, sabre-rattling secularization imposed by Napoleon in 1803. In the last instance, Napoleon annexed German territories on the left bank of the Rhine and 'compensated' the States on the right bank with land he confiscated from the Catholic Church. In other words, he took something that was not his and 'paid' for it with something he had seized from somebody else.

Secularization, no doubt, represented a bad blow to the wealth of the Catholic Church in Germany on immediate terms. It lost the estates belonging to four archdioceses, eight dioceses, eighty abbeys and over two thousand monasteries. For the Laender concerned, however (considering it on a strictly territorial, business basis, not on a political or nationalist one), this was not a bad deal after all. It has been reckoned that Bavaria got seven times more land than it had lost in the forced swap, while Prussia and Wuerttenberg got about four times more.

But the whole question is rather involved both from the juridical and the moral point of view. It could be asked whether it is right for the German State to make its citizens pay at the present time for the consequences of an illegal action committed by Napoleon in 1803.

Anyhow, it is quite understandable that the two churches should defend to the utmost the privileged position they hold today. Should the Kirchensteuer and all the other State contributions, that is 90 per cent of their revenues, stop from one day to the next, both confessions would face almost immediate bankruptcy. No wonder, therefore, that the two main German churches should have joined forces to maintain the status quo. A typical episode took place when the Constitutional Court ruled on 14 December 1965 that a person who was neither a Catholic nor a Protestant, but who was married to a professed Catholic or Protestant, should not be subjected to the Kirchensteuer. It also ruled that juridical persons, registered companies for instance, should be exempted from paying a tax towards church building programmes which was in force in Baden. Immediately the two representatives of Catholic and Protestant finances, that is the Catholic vicar-general of the archdiocese of Freiburg, Dr Föhr, and the Finanzreferent Der Evangelische Landeskirche Baden, Dr Löhr, got together. Föhr and Löhr presented the Baden-Wuerttenberg region with the following bill : DM 20 million a year for the loss of the tax for church building and DM 72 million to be paid once and for all as a compensation for the loss of other sources of revenue caused by the ruling of the Constitutional Court.

But if one looks at the question in a more general perspective, keeping in mind spiritual values, one may wonder whether the German system does not have some disadvantages. On the one hand, this impersonal, automatic way of contributing money to the church through the tax collector weakens the bonds between the faithful and their priests. On the other hand, the priests, being assured of a steady income guaranteed by the State, almost inevitably tend to fall into routine, to acquire a bureaucratic rather than pastoral mentality. More and more priests are becoming entirely absorbed in administrative posts and the rest spend more and more time on paper work and in supervising building. There are at present in West Germany about 20,000 secular priests (with an approximate rate of one priest to 1,348 Catholics); it has been reckoned that 30 per cent are taken up with administrative jobs, teaching, or running newspapers, magazines or cultural activities, and that the remaining 70 per cent who are engaged in pastoral work have to devote 40 per cent of their time to paper work and the supervision of buildings.

The passion for building, which borders on mania, and which, if one looks at the city of Rome, can be considered typical of the Catholic Church, has affected the level-headed German clergy as well. From the end of the war to 1961 no less than 1,100 new churches have been built in West Germany (costing an average of one million each as against the half million of prefabricated churches adopted in the dioceses of Essen and Rottenburg), i.e., more churches than in the preceding four hundred years. Speaking in general terms, one can say that practically the entire Kirchensteuer and the other State subsidies and regional and communal contributions are absorbed by the salaries of the clergy, closely followed by building expenses. There is very little margin left for other initiatives.

The salaries, without being extravagant, are substantial as far as the higher and middle section of the hierarchy is concerned. A bishop gets about 3,000 marks a month and a priest with a certain seniority about 1,500. The picture is not as rosy on the lower rungs of the ladder : a chaplain, besides free food and lodging, receives only 300 marks a month, after having completed his theological studies at the age of twenty-seven. He must wait another seventeen years—on average, naturally—before becoming a parish priest and moving to a higher-income bracket.

As our main scope was that of tracing the sources of income of the Catholic Church in general, we should like once more to underline the fact that the West Germans are the second best contributors to Catholic initiatives immediately after the United States Catholics. If one took into account the Kirchensteuer also and all the other more or less indirect contributions, which can be roughly evaluated at $300 million a year, they might even be given first place.

We have already mentioned when dealing with Propaganda Fide that in 1966 Misereor collected 56 million marks and Adveniat 48 million.[3] We can now add, excluding Caritas Internationalis and many other similar activities, that the German Catholics responded to the 1965–66 campaign against hunger (*Brot fuer die Welt*) with no less than 20.9 million.

Most German Catholics I have spoken to on this matter did not seem to realise how much they were already contributing to their church, somewhat automatically and unconsciously, through the tax collector. Or, if they did, they seemed to take it for granted, as something quite normal. This might explain their additional generosity towards other national and international fund-raising concerns.

But it is far from being an entirely satisfactory explanation. An easy and valid counter-argument is the fact that the German Protestant Church, which outnumbers the Catholics and which pays more Kirchensteuer, contributes to the three-yearly fund-raising collections for national and international missionary initiatives only a paltry 1.5 million a year. It just shows that, while in Germany also religion in general faces its most dangerous enemy, indifference,

[3] Since its foundation, German Catholics have contributed to Adveniat over 256 million marks.

the Catholic Church is less affected by this and practising Catholics still respond with considerable eagerness to the appeals of their clergy.

13

The Scene Is Changing

As we are approaching the end of our survey of the intricate and elusive world of Vatican finances, one may just as well try and draw some conclusions. The overall picture is full of lights and shadows. The lights are represented by the good the Catholic Church is doing in the areas of education, culture, medical care and welfare and by the fact that most of the money is provided by the spontaneous, generous donations of millions of Catholics. The Church of Rome has proved to be a very worthy instrument for provoking and collecting an impressive flow of charity. This is then re-distributed to those who need it with efficiency, wisdom and with the minimum of waste and of overhead expenses. Parkinson's laws do not apply to the Vatican.

The shadows concern the difficulty of reconciling the image of the Pope as the representative of Christ on earth with that of a temporal ruler and the ruler of a vast financial empire. To reconcile the definition of the Roman Catholic Church as 'the Church of the Poor'—a definition which Pope Paul often repeats—with the big business in which she is deeply involved; the ideal of poverty of St Francis of Assisi with the fluctuations of the stock exchange. Naturally, those who run the finances of the Holy See are not out to make a personal profit, but to gain money in order to use it to spread the Gospel and for humanitarian purposes. But it is hard to accept that so much Vatican capital should be invested to build luxury hotels, residential quarters with golf courses and swimming pools, and that it should make a profit out of the shares of Radio Corporation of America, Italy's biggest maker of dance music records. The situation becomes ironical when one considers that the Istituto Farmacologico Serono (pharmaceuticals), in which the Vatican is interested, is currently making the pill which the Pope has condemned. Officially the pill is still banned in Italy, enforcing a Fascist law against birth control which has not yet been repealed, but in practice it is sold freely by all chemists under the name of *Luteolas* and the disguise of a medicine to cure gynaecological complaints. One cannot help wondering whether the Pope knows. It is equally disconcerting to recall that when Mgr Agostino Casaroli, the Secretariat of State official who specializes in negotiations with the Communist countries, concluded an agreement with Hungary in 1964, he managed to convince the Hungarian Government to buy sanitary appliances from the Vatican controlled Ceramica Pozzi which was in difficulties. Vatican diplomacy boosting the sales of lavatories. But, as Emperor Vespasian said when he was criticized for making money out of cesspools : *'Pecunia non olet'*. (Money doesn't stink.)

Another reason for criticism is the fact that the running of Vatican finances has been, and to a considerable degree still is, the monopoly of a restricted group of Italians who either belong to the Black Aristocracy or were favoured by nepotism—see the three Pacelli brothers. The whole system still smacks of feudalism. But, as we shall soon see, things seem to be changing in this particular field.

When we turn to Vatican investments outside Italy we find an even greater contradiction between the official doctrine of the Church of Rome, as embodied in the encyclical *Populorum progressio*, and her current financial practices. The encyclical strongly condemns liberal capitalism, but the Vatican, as a financial entity, has close ties with such archcapitalistic institutions as the Rothschilds of France, Britain and America, Hambros Bank in Britain, the Crédit Suisse in Zurich and London, and, across the Atlantic, the Chase Manhattan Bank, the Bankers Trust Company, the First National Bank of New York and the Morgan Bank. It also owns shares in several of the world's giant international corporations including General Motors, Shell, Gulf Oil, General Electric, Bethlehem Steel, International Business Machines, TWA, and also in the less international New York Central Railroad. The total amount of the Holy See investments in the United States has been valued by the Vatican correspondent Giampaolo Jorio, nephew of the late Cardinal Domenico Jorio, at more than £30 million.

Where financing exists on this scale, direct investment is only half the picture. It is in the nature of giant corporations that they in turn invest in other companies, either to extend markets, to gain control in certain areas of operation, or to collaborate over manufacture, market and development. The influence of any major block of investment capital extends well beyond its immediate recipient, and the profits realized on such investment are drawn from a far wider area than the operations of the corporation in which shares are held.

A great deal more is involved than the simple business of sitting on blocks of profitable shares. The big shareholders take part in the general manoeuvring for position in world markets. Since Vatican nominees hold important, and often the most important, places on directorial boards, it is vital to any understanding of the ramifications of papal finance to consider the interlocking shareholding between companies in which the Vatican has a direct interest and those with which such companies are associated. Let us look briefly at some of these operating in Great Britain.

One corporation in which the Vatican has a large direct interest is SNIA-Viscosa, a huge textile group concentrating on artificial fibres and plastics and on all the chemical industries that surround their production. Massimo Spada is the man on the board who looks after Vatican interests. This company has two London directors; their names are Colonel Francis Thomas Davies and Mr Cecil Wilfred Sheldon. The latter is also a director of the British textile giant, Courtaulds.

Within the SNIA-Viscosa network in Italy are a very large number of companies, among which are two other textile firms—Interfan and Novaceta. The first of these is actually a subsidiary of British Courtaulds; the second an associate company.

In London the financial agents for SNIA-Viscosa are Hambros Bank. Hambros also has an Italian associated company—the Banca Privata Finanziaria. Hambros investment affairs are controlled by another subsidiary called Westminster Hambros Trust Ltd., owned jointly and equally by Hambros and the Westminster Bank.

Massimo Spada is on the board of Shell Italiana, which is an associate of the Shell Transport and Trading Company Ltd., the British financial company controlling the British share of the Royal Dutch Shell group. There is thus a direct financial connection between Shell Italiana and the British firm.

All the money the Special Administration had in Britain was at one time invested in Empire bonds. This goes back to an episode in 1948 when the Catholic Relief Organization in Germany received several shiploads of wheat which the Vatican had bought in the Argentine. The wheat was paid for by Bernardino Nogara with money the Special Administration had banked in England. The British, who were still under a regime of austerity and currency restrictions, were naturally annoyed. There were negotiations between the British Exchequer and the Holy See, and Nogara agreed to invest the money he had in England in British State bonds. And this, as far as I know, could still be the case.

The secrecy surrounding the finances of the Vatican has given rise to two legends. The first, as we already saw, concerns the fabulous wealth of the Holy See. The lack of data has induced most writers on this subject to exaggerate—in doubt—more in excess than in defect. A typical example is that of Nino Lo Bello, an American writer, author of the generally well-informed book *Vatican Empire*.[1] In it he reached the amazing conclusion that the Vatican owned 'between 40 and 50 per cent of the total number of shares quoted on all the Italian stock exchanges'. He then reckoned that this means that the Vatican owns in Italy alone shares worth about $5 billion. This statement would appear to be an exaggeration when one considers that nearly 70 per cent of all Italian shares are owned by over one million small investors. The remaining 30 per cent is in the hands of a few hundred financiers and industrialists including such giants as Agnelli, Pirelli, Volpi, Cini, Olivetti, Valerio, Pesenti, Marzotto, Crespi, Mondadori, Samaritani, Feltrinelli, Falk, Cicogna, Sindona (to mention just a few) . . . and of the Vatican. If it were true that the Vatican owned 40 per cent of the shares, let alone 50 per cent, there simply wouldn't be any room left for the million small investors, nor for the financial giants, nor for the supergiants represented by the State-controlled IRI, ENEL (nationalized electricity) and ENI (oil and natural gas).

One must also remember that the Vatican doesn't own all, and not even nearly all, the shares of the companies it controls. In Italy, as in most other countries, the ownership of between 10 per cent and 20 per cent of the shares (very often much less) is quite enough

[1] Trident Press (US and Canada, 1968).

to control the company, mainly because the bulk of the shareholders, that is the small investors, are not organized and hardly ever attend the company meetings. A good example is that of Immobiliare which the Vatican has been strictly controlling for many decades by owning only 15 per cent of the shares. In view of all this, and even if one didn't trust the official figure of 100 billion lire given by the Socialist Finance Minister Luigi Preti as representing the total amount of Vatican capital invested in Italian shares, one should divide Lo Bello's assessment at least by ten. Also, can anybody imagine a Finance Minister, even the most bigoted of all Christian Democrat Finance Ministers, exempting from between 40 and 50 per cent of all Italian shares from tax, on the pretext that they belonged to the Vatican?

Another point on which I must reluctantly disagree with Nino Lo Bello concerns the Vatican bank. On page 37 of *Vatican Empire* he refers to it as 'the now abolished Institute for Religious Works'. It must have been a slip of the pen or a printer's error, because the Institute for Religious Works, far from having been abolished, is very much alive and has become, if anything, the chief instrument of Vatican finances. It owns more shares in Italy than all the other Vatican financial offices combined and has closer ties with the big international banks abroad. Its importance and independence has been underlined by the fact that the Pope has removed it from the supervision of the new Prefecture for Economic Affairs. It has remained autonomous.

The second legend surrounding Vatican finances concerns the shrewdness of its operators. The Vatican financiers, both clergy and laity, have often been credited by the press, especially the Anglo-American press, with an almost infallible flair for business, as if they possessed a magic wand which turned into gold whatever they touched. But this is not true. On the contrary, while the portfolio investments have usually been sound, the direct investments have often gone wrong. The first big post-war flop was the Cotonificio Majno (textiles) in which the Vatican owned the controlling shares and which had to be sold to Cotonificio Olcese at a very heavy loss. Also the Molini Biondi (flour) and the Pastificio Pantanella (spaghetti), in which the Vatican has a direct investment, have been losing a great deal of money, particularly the latter whose president is Prince Marcantonio Pacelli. Another company we mentioned before, the Ceramica Pozzi (sanitary appliances), has tried to branch off, too fast and too rashly, into many other areas including petro-chemical products, and had to be rescued by Immobiliare.

But what are the prospects of the Vatican financial empire? Will it remain a fundamentally Italian affair, with the bulk of the investments made in Italy and run primarily by Italian ecclesiastics, Italian princes, counts, barons and relatives and protégés of the Popes? Will secrecy remain the rule? To all these questions my answer is in the negative. Changes are already taking place.

One general trend is that of reducing the almost Byzantine pomp surrounding the person of the Pope and of gradually eliminating the anachronistic Papal Court. Most of the more preposterous titles, such as Secret Chamberlain of Sword and Cape, Secret Chamberlain Participating, Secret Sweeper, Major Master of the Horses, Bearer of the Golden Rose, Honorary Chamberlain in Scarlet Habit, etc., and even the Noble Guard, have either been abolished outright or are left to fade out by not replacing their holders as they die. The ties between the Pope and the big aristocratic Roman families are getting weaker and will eventually disappear completely.

But the whole Catholic Church, as one knows, has, since the stimulating reign of Pope John and the equally stimulating Ecumenical Council, started changing at all levels. It has become less dogmatic, less authoritarian, more open to new ideas and to debate, more public relations conscious and, in a way, more democratic. It is certainly not my task nor intention to go into all this, but I would like to quote just two episodes. Before the Ecumenical Council it would have been inconceivable for a Cardinal, as Cardinal Suenens of Belgium did recently, to state in an interview that the spirit of the Council had been betrayed by the Roman Curia, that the next Pope should not be elected by the Sacred College of Cardinals but by all the Bishops and that it would be a good idea if the Vatican abandoned the pretence of being a political, temporal power and abolished its diplomatic representatives abroad, that is the Nuncios. And Suenens is certainly not a sensation-seeking, soap-box orator, but a highly respected leader of the progressive wing of the Catholic episcopate with not indifferent chances of being the next Pope. It would have been equally inconceivable until a few years ago for 774 French priests, friars and workers to address a letter to the Pope, which happened in December 1968, urging him to demolish St Peter's Basilica as a 'monument of ecclesiastic pride, a testimonial of the shameful commerce of indulgences and a reminder of the days in which the Popes were only intent on building works of art without bothering with the schisms that were tearing the Church apart'. (An obvious reference to Leo X, Martin Luther and the Protestant Reform.) I'm certainly not implying that, should Suenens or an equally progressive Cardinal succeed Pope Paul on the throne of Peter, he would demolish St Peter's to please the 774 French romantics; I am merely suggesting that he would approach the question of Vatican finances from a different, more rational, less secretive, less nepotistic, and in the end probably even more profitable, point of view.

The gradual internationalization of the Roman Curia has already affected the administration of the finances of the Holy See. The Secretary of State, who has become more and more the Pope's right hand man, used traditionally to be an Italian. The last non-Italian Secretary of State was the brilliant English Cardinal of Spanish origin Merry del Val (1913). But here, too, things have changed. The present Secretary of State is the French Cardinal Jean Villot, who also supervizes, *ex officio*, the Administration of the Patrimony of the Holy See (which now includes the former Special Administration) and the Administration of the Vatican City State, plus the Pius XII Foundation for the Apostolate of Laymen, as well as Peter's Pence and all the funds of the State Secretariat. Pope Paul has appointed Mgr Paul Marcinkus as secretary of the Vatican bank, that is the Institute for Religious Works. He is a shrewd, gigantic, golf-playing American who rose to prominence because of his flair for languages and his ability in organizing the Pope's trips abroad. Yet another American, Cardinal John Joseph Wright, the former Bishop of Pittsburgh, has become the Prefect of the Congregation of the Clergy, which also handles a considerable amount of money. I would not be too surprised if, with the decline of nepotism and of the Black Aristocracy, with the spreading of a more modern outlook and with the presence of one Frenchman and three Americans in key financial positions, the strategy of Vatican investments should expand on a wider international field.

There are already straws in the wind. The Rothschilds, who were lending money to the Holy See in 1831 and who have kept good financial relations with it ever since, have again appeared on the scene. During the month of June 1969, the Vatican sold to the Parisbas Transcompany of Luxembourg, which is controlled by the powerful Banque de Paris et des Pays Bas, which in turn belongs to the French branch of the Rothschilds, the controlling shares of Immobiliare. The move was preceded by a foray on Immobiliare by the Sicilian financier Michele Sindona, a lawyer who operates mostly in the field of real estate from his Milan headquarters. Sindona has many strong international connections and he is president of Keyes Italiana, Rotostar, Merx, Tyndaris (sweets), Mediterranean Holidays, Phillips Carbon Black Italiana, vice-president of Banca Finanziaria Privata, managing director of Chesebrough Pond's Italiana, on the board of Remington Rand Italiana, Reeves Italiana, SNIA-Viscosa, and syndic of Vickers. Quite recently Sindona has bought from the Assicurazioni Generali, one of the main shareholders of Immobiliare, a packet representing 3.5 per cent of all the shares and this has gained him an appointment on the board of directors on 14 June 1969. Sindona is also closely connected with Hambros Bank and with the Continental Bank of Illinois, presided over by Mr David Kennedy, the United States Treasury Minister. One could also recall that the present President of the French Republic, Georges Pompidou, worked for many years for the private bank of the Rothschilds. An interesting and perhaps significant detail is that Mgr Marcinkus, secretary of the Institute for Religious Works and the new *éminence grise* of Vatican finance, was born in Cicero, Illinois. But what is the percentage of Immobiliare shares now controlled by the Rothschilds? Although no figures have been disclosed, this can be easily worked out. Before the sale to Parisbas the Vatican owned 15 per cent of the Immobiliare shares. Shortly after the sale the official spokesman of the Vatican, Mgr Fausto Vallainc, said in a press conference that the Vatican participation in the company was of approximately 5 per cent. This would mean that 10 per cent was sold to Parisbas.

The Vatican has also recently sold 20 per cent of the shares of Condotte d'Acqua to Bastogi and 5 per cent to the Banque de Paris et des Pays Bas which already had a participation in this once Vatican-controlled company. It was left with 12.5 per cent, but according to the latest information gathered in financial quarters, this too was subsequently sold to the Rothschilds. The Condotte d'Acqua, as we already saw, is presided over by Marquis Giovanni Battista Sacchetti, it has a capital of 7 billion lire and it specializes in aqueducts, tunnels and public works on a big scale. Bastogi, with a capital of 1 billion lire, is a financial company the ownership of which is shared by some of the biggest Italian concerns including Montedison, Pirelli, Fiat, the Bank of Italy, Assicurazioni Generali, La Fondiaria, the Sviluppo, Mediobanca, La Centrale, Italcementi, Sindona and the Vatican. It is reported that none of them own more than 4 per cent of the shares. It appears that the *deus ex machina* of these intricate transactions is Michele Sindona. Acting either on his own behalf or that of the Rothschilds or of David Kennedy, he has been quietly buying up a lot of shares of Italcementi, the kingdom of Pesenti. In the beginning Pesenti was not alarmed, because he felt protected by his alliance with the Vatican. But then he realized that Sindona was going a bit too far and might acquire control of the whole cement monopoly. He ordered his own banks to buy Italcementi shares to strengthen his position. At present the battle is still going on with Sindona owning 15 per cent of the shares, Pesenti 10 per cent or 12 per cent and the Vatican holding the balance with 7.35 per cent.

But why is the Vatican pulling out of the Italian market or, at least, reducing its involvements? There are many explanations, but three main points can possibly provide a satisfactory answer.

Firstly, to be cynical, there are now in the world many more profitable and safe ways of investing money than sinking it into Italian companies. For instance, while the Immobiliare shares give a profit of 3.97 per cent, Italcementi only 1.68 per cent and Assicurazioni Generali a mere 0.72 per cent, one can easily obtain an interest of 8 per cent by opening a deposit account in a Swiss bank, not to mention the higher yields of the Investment Funds.

Secondly, to be idealistic, the Vatican might feel that to be involved in building luxury hotels, residential quarters for the very rich, selling the pill to the Italians or sanitary appliances to the Hungarian Communists, was not quite in keeping with the image of herself the Church wants to project. Also to be noted that recently the Italian press has taken to probing into Vatican investments and that the revelation of the vastness of Vatican penetration into the country's economy was unfavourably received by the man in the street and was a source of embarrassment to Catholic politicians. More anodyne investments in countries other than Italy would cause less controversy.

Third, again being cynical, the fact that the Vatican did not manage to get exempted from paying taxes on the Italian shares might also have influenced the decision to look for greener pastures.

Things are moving and I cannot help feeling that, if somebody should attempt another survey of the financial empire of the Vatican in ten years' time, he would find the overall picture considerably changed : more rational, more international and less secretive.

APPENDIX

'Go sell whatsoever thou hast, and give to
the poor, and thou shalt have treasure in
heaven.'

Mark 10:21

Reading again, in August 1970, what I had written at the end of
1969, I realise that I had been a bit too cautious. Things have
moved, and continue to move, in the directions I had indicated,
but much faster than I had predicted.

First of all the Pope himself has openly recognised the contradiction existing between the ideal of poverty preached by Christ
and the wealth, or the supposed wealth and its appearances, of the
Holy See. In the second place the Vatican, in an effort to dispel
the legend of fabulous riches, has lifted, if only partly and
cautiously, the veil of secrecy surrounding its finances. In the third
place the process of reorganising Vatican finances on a more
modern and rational basis and getting out of too direct, nepotistic
and embarrassing dealings has been pushed several steps forward.

The Pope's speech was delivered in the course of a general
audience held in St Peter's on 24 June 1970. He began by quoting
a famous phrase of Pope John : 'The Church presents herself as
she is, as she wants to be, as the Church of everybody and particularly as the Church of the Poor.' He then plunged into long-
winded praise of the concept of poverty as expressed by the birth,
the life and the teaching of Christ, as if it were something newly
discovered. There followed a rather lame attempt to justify the
temporal power exercised and the huge wealth enjoyed by the
Church of Rome throughout the centuries.

Finally, coming to the present, Pope Paul firmly stated : 'The
Church must be poor and appear to be poor.' He then explained :

One could easily demonstrate that the fabulous wealth, which now and then certain public opinion attributes to her, is of a quite different nature, often insufficient to the modest and legitimate needs of ordinary life, to the needs of so many ecclesiastics and religious and of beneficent and pastoral institutions. But we don't want to make this apology now. Let us instead accept the desire which today's men, especially those who look at the Church from the outside, feel for the Church to manifest herself as she should be : certainly not as an economic power, not appearing to have great wealth, not engaged in financial speculations, not indifferent to the needs of indigent persons, institutions and nations. We notice with vigilant attention that, in a period like ours which is completely taken up by the acquisition, the possession and the enjoyment of material goods, one feels that public opinion, both inside and outside the Church, desires to see the poverty of the Gospel and that it wants to recognise this even more where the Gospel is preached and represented : in the official Church, in our own Apostolic See. We are aware of this exigency, internal and external, of our ministry. And just as, by the grace of God, many things have already been accomplished to renounce temporal power and to reform the style of the Church, so we shall proceed, with the respect due to legitimate *de facto* situations, but with the confidence of being understood by the faithful, in our effort to overcome situations which do not conform with the spirit and the good of the true Church.

Does this mean that the Pope is determined to carry out Christ's command : 'Go sell whatsoever thou hast, and give to the poor'? Some marginal episodes seemed to confirm this simple, straightforward interpretation. Mgr Fausto Vallainc (before he was consecrated bishop and replaced as Vatican spokesman by Doctor Alessandrini, vice-editor of *Osservatore Romano*), having announced a 10 per cent raise of all salaries and wages of Vatican employees, added that, in order to face the supplementary expense, the Holy See had to sell shares and properties. A case of charity beginning at home? Mgr Vallainc did not explain which shares nor which real estate had been sold. According to our calculations (see page 84), a 10 per cent increase represents about $1 million a year. As for the sale of real estate, it was reported that this included the vast Collegio Pio Latino-Americano on the outskirts of Rome, which was completed only five years ago and which remained to a large extent unused. Reportedly it has been bought, for the sum of three billion lire ($4,840,000), by a United States cultural institution.

As for the sale of shares, we mentioned in the preceding chapter that the Vatican had sold the controlling shares of Generale Immobiliare, the company in which it was most deeply involved, to Parisbas. It was subsequently learnt that Parisbas had been buying on behalf of the United States tycoon Charles Bludhorn, the forty-four-year-old president of Gulf & Western which, among many other concerns, owns the Paramount Film Company. In June 1970 Bludhorn and one of his associates, thirty-six-year-old Don Goston, were appointed to the board of Immobiliare. The Vatican also had shares in Condotte d'Acqua which were sold to Parisbas. The Vatican has also sold its shares in Ceramica Pozzi and Molini e Pastificio Pantanella. The latter, with Prince Marcantonio Pacelli as its president, was going from bad to worse and has been bought up by a big American investment fund, the Equity Funding of Los Angeles.

It is, therefore, certain that the Vatican is selling. But selling to 'give to the poor'? To implement the Pope's dictum that 'the Church must be poor and appear to be poor'? Or to re-invest? The answers to these questions were provided by statements made by Cardinal Egidio Vagnozzi, the head of the Prefecture for Economic Affairs, and by Mgr Giuseppe Caprio, the newly appointed secretary of the Administration of the Patrimony of the Apostolic See, to the American journalist Paul Horne. Both of them outlined the new strategy of Vatican finances in more or less the same words. The overall picture certainly wasn't that of renouncing the wealth of the Vatican in a Quixotical sort of way just to make the Church poor, but rather that of employing the existing resources in a more rational way in order to *increase* the output of capital.

Cardinal Vagnozzi said:

When the Pope explained that we need more money and are a poor Church, he meant exactly that! We, the managers, want to improve investment performance, balanced of course against what must be a fundamentally conservative investment philosophy. It wouldn't do for the Church to lose its principal in speculation. This is even more important as major currencies depreciate and costs rise. We have decided to avoid attempting to maintain control of companies in which we invest, as was done in the past. The financial responsibility of the Holy See for such companies has to be reduced. We are thus diversifying our investments over a larger number of companies, while reducing our holdings to minority positions. This means getting away from the traditional practice of lay Vatican fiduciaries sitting on the boards of companies in which we invested. The Vatican simply cannot afford primary responsibility for business failures requiring transfusions of capital. We do not want to commit the Church to only a few companies, nor to a single investment field, nor even a single national economy. We are reducing our real estate holdings and increasing securities investments. The Vatican's investment policy remains basically conservative, although the Church's increasing needs mean that the balance between conservation and the need to increase income has been moving towards the need to increase income. We are, to put it simply, more performance minded now.

Echoing Cardinal Vagnozzi, Mgr Caprio, who before being appointed secretary of the Administration had spent twenty-three years in the Far East and had been Apostolic Internuncio to Formosa, said:

Controlling interest in a company is no longer necessary. Modern stock markets have made it possible to have safe investments without control of the company's management. Today our investment criteria are the following: security of principal; increase of income, and, since market ups and downs are inevitable, speculation is strictly avoided. It is not true that we are withdrawing from the Italian market. But we are shifting funds around in an effort to diversify. We do not have a specific policy to liquidate in Italy and invest abroad.

All this means that the era of the Vatican as a business manager directly involved in running this or that company is finished; it means that nepotism, both in the literal and the wider sense of the word, is definitely on the way out.[1] Working in simply-furnished, modernly-equipped offices hidden behind the ornate doors of Raphael's magnificent Loggias, and quite close to the Pope's own official reception quarters, a small team of clerical and lay investment analysts, each of them a specialist in a particular field, is following, on a day to day basis, the fluctuations of industrial shares, securities and State bonds the Vatican owns in many countries. By pressing a button they can get the latest quotations on the stock markets of the City, Wall Street, Zurich or Milan. They also evaluate the specific recommendations of leading financial institutions such as Hambros Bank, the Morgan Guarantee Trust Company, the Rothschilds, the Bankers Trust and firms of brokers such as Merrill Lynch and Bache, and check them against their own confidential information. The Vatican, as a financial entity, is operating more and more like a big investment fund with conservative leanings. And it will thus become even more elusive, as the presence of a Vatican fiduciary on the board of a company will no longer necessarily mean that the Holy See has money invested in it. The mystery will thicken, unless, of course, the Holy See finally decides to publish its budget so that, to use the words of *Civiltà Cattolica*, the magazine of the Jesuits, 'the Church would gain credibility if its administration became a glass house into which all could easily look'. However, two and a half years after the creation of the Prefecture for Economic Affairs, and one and a half years after he took over, Cardinal Vagnozzi had to confess that, because of the intricate and scattered ways of accounting of the various organisations, he still hadn't been able to produce a consolidated balance sheet.

At this point the justly irritated reader may well ask : but how wealthy *is* the Vatican? How much money does it have? Some light has been thrown on this subject by an article in the *Osservatore Romano* of 22 July 1970. It was provoked by Nino Lo Bello's book which (as I noted on pages 162–3) contained some evident exaggerations. The *Osservatore Romano* recalled that the *Tribune de Lausanne*, summarising Lo Bello's book, had written that 'the productive capital of the Vatican can be reckoned at between 50

---

[1] Prince Carlo Pacelli, who figured prominently as an example of nepotism, died on 7 August 1970. Cardinal Pizzardo, one of the 'Old Guard', died on 1 August 1970, aged ninety-three.

and 55 billion Swiss francs, that is 7,000–8,000 billion lire.' To this the Vatican organ angrily replied : 'It is a simply fantastic figure. In reality, the productive capital of the Holy See, including both deposits and investments, placed both in Italy and outside Italy, is far from reaching one hundredth of this sum.' We still do not have a precise figure, but at least we have a ceiling. If Lo Bello's figure is divided by a hundred we shall get minus 70 billion lire (£46 million or $111 million). Is it a plausible figure?

We may recall that in 1968 Finance Minister Luigi Preti (see page 124) had officially assessed Vatican investments in Italy alone at about 100 billion lire. This did not include investments in other countries nor bank deposits in Italy and elsewhere. But before we accuse the Vatican of lying, we must hasten to say that *Osservatore Romano* has not taken into account the assets of the Vatican bank, which Preti included in his calculations. 'The figure of 7,000–8,000 billion lire,' the Vatican newspaper explained, 'represents a fantastic exaggeration even if one should consider activities pertaining to institutions which have particular aims, among which is the Institute for Religious Works.' And as we already saw (page 124), the Institute owned more Italian shares than all the other Vatican organisations combined. One may also add that the Institute, that is the bank of the Vatican, like any other bank holds and administers the deposits of its clients, that is of religious orders, Catholic schools, hospitals, cultural institutions, diplomats accredited to the Holy See, Vatican citizens, etc., on behalf of the clients and that the income of the capital cannot be used to meet the expenses of the central administration of the Catholic Church. One can, therefore, accept the *Osservatore Romano* statement that the productive capital of the Vatican is less than one hundredth of the figures mentioned by Lo Bello.

But in order to get a clearer idea of the actual wealth of the Vatican, to the income of productive capital one must add many other sources of income, like the rents from Vatican-owned buildings, Peter's Pence, donations, legacies, the sale of stamps and of tickets to the Vatican Museums, profits made by the duty-free shops, the sale of souvenirs, etc. What it all amounts to nobody so far, not even Cardinal Vagnozzi, has been able or willing to reveal.

To return to Vatican investments, *Osservatore Romano*, in order to refute Lo Bello, has let a few more facts and figures slip out. It stated that the Vatican has never owned shares of Lancia, not even before Pesenti sold it to Fiat, and that it doesn't own either Alfa Romeo or Italcementi shares. It didn't say whether it owned them in the past. It also said that the Vatican holding in Italgas is 0.92 per cent, and less than 1 per cent in snia-Viscosa and Montedison. *Osservatore Romano* then denied the statement by the *Tribune de Lausanne* according to which 'the Holy See is one of the main shareholders of iri'. This, the Vatican newspaper pointed out, is impossible for the simple reason that iri is a State-owned holding which has no *shares* nor shareholders. Technically, it's absolutely correct. But it doesn't prevent the Vatican owning iri *bonds*, which yield a good interest, are tax free and guaranteed by the State. According to my information the Vatican has quite a lot of them. As for the unofficial but very strong personal links between iri and the Vatican through men who hold key positions in both administrations, we have already pointed them out on page 109.

Apart from these interesting but minor details, the *Osservatore Romano* made a fundamental statement, namely that, after the sale of the Immobiliare shares, 'the Holy See doesn't own the controlling shares of any company'. It confirms that the new policy of diversification of investments outlined by Cardinal Vagnozzi is well under way. The Vatican is not yet a glass house into which everybody can look, it still is a considerable financial power and is likely to remain so, but the legend of its wealth has been reduced to more realistic proportions and many of the unpleasant shadows that surrounded its dealings have started to fade away.

INDEX